NEW DIRECTIONS
FOR THE
COMPREHENSIVE HIGH SCHOOL

NEW DIRECTIONS
FOR THE
COMPREHENSIVE HIGH SCHOOL

B. Frank Brown

Parker Publishing Company

West Nyack, New York

Library of Congress Cataloging in Publication Data

Brown, Bartley Frank, **(date)**
    New directions for the comprehensive high school.

    Includes bibliographical references.
    1. High schools--United States. 2. Non-graded
schools. I. Title.
LA222.B86   373.2'5   72-3975
ISBN 0-13-612309-0

Printed in the United States of America

IN MEMORIAM

This book is dedicated to the memory of Charles F. Kettering II, whose vital and compassionate commitment to the esteem of the individual in the learning process will be a prevailing inspiration and legacy to the field of education.

Other books by the author:

Education by Appointment: New Approaches to Independent
Study

Appropriate Placement School: A Sophisticated Nongraded
Curriculum

The Origin and Objectives
of This Book ...

James B. Conant's book *The American High School Today,* first published in 1959, has had more impact on the organization and operation of the nation's high schools than any happening since 1918 when the seven cardinal principles of education were formulated.

Like any piece of writing over ten years old and dealing with education, the Conant study is now hopelessly out of date. This is one of the reasons for the writing of a new book on the high school, its curriculum, and its organization. So, this study is an effort to update what should be happening in today's high schools and at the same time point to some new directions.

Let me state from the outset that my own career as a high school principal has been greatly influenced by the Conant study and Dr. Conant's collaborator in writing it, Eugene Youngert.

The idea for this book came to me when I was a participant in the Ditchley, England, seminar on the Comprehensive High School. This Anglo-American conference of educators was convened by the Ditchley Foundation for the express purpose of examining developments in comprehensive high schools in England and the United States.

What struck me most about this conference was the advanced state of the development of the British Comprehensive High School. Circular 1065 from the National Department of Education requires that all British high schools develop comprehensiveness.

After studying the British version of this institution in considerable depth, I raised the question with Dr. Conant as to why he had disregarded the British effort, which was in a high state of development when his book was published, and had been for twenty years. He responded that "the Comprehensive High School is strictly an American invention," and his position was unassailable. There is no question but what there is more emphasis on comprehensiveness today in Britain than in the United States and the principles of the British Comprehensive High School are much more highly developed than their U.S. counterpart. Whether Dr. Conant was correct in disregarding this effort is a matter for history to decide. In my opinion it amounted to a serious factual and historical error.

While I have the greatest admiration for Dr. Conant and his work, as a practicing educator he espoused several principles with which I profoundly disagree. These will be discussed briefly.

Dr. Conant established three objectives for the Comprehensive High School. These are:

(1) to provide a general education for all of the future citizens;
(2) to provide good elective programs for those who wish to use their acquired skills immediately on graduation;
(3) to provide satisfactory programs for those whose vocations will depend on their subsequent education.

I am convinced that the Conant objective of general education is inappropriate to the youth of today. The explosion of knowledge, coupled with the new emphasis on specialization, makes it unnecessary for a high school to provide a general education.

The modern comprehensive school should have three major programs:

(1) a strong academic program for youngsters who plan to attend a college or university on graduation;
(2) a viable vocational program which will provide students with the necessary skills for earning a living in one of the trades immediately upon graduation;
(3) an effective skills program for students in need of remedial work in reading, writing, or mathematics.

Dr. Conant expressed grave concern about the matter of establishing interaction between students of different abilities and those with varying vocational goals. This problem doesn't bother me at all. While nearly everyone agrees with the lovely statement of John Gardner's that "we must show respect for both our philosophers and our plumbers or neither our pipes nor our philosophy will hold water," few of us know of cases where philosophers and plumbers mix in life after high school. Why should we force an unrealistic and uncomfortable association on public school youth when this is not the society in which they will live? In essence, the school must accommodate an amalgamation of students and provide a diversification of opportunities. It does not, and should not, encroach upon the individual's mores and choice of associates.

Another point on which I vigorously disagree with Dr. Conant is the matter of homerooms. In his report, Dr. Conant specified well-organized homerooms as an essential appurtenance of the comprehensive school. The homeroom organization is one of the monumental failures in secondary education. Consequently, I do not advocate this philosophy in the comprehensive high school, nor do I agree that this is an essential component in the development of a democratic spirit.

I do most decisively agree with the notion of the development of a democratic spirit but believe that this should be implemented in more viable situations than the homeroom. A democratic spirit is more easily acquired in after-school activities, physical education classes, field work, art, music, and courses which cater to an individual's special talents.

The function of the homeroom as an administrative device for announcements, elections, etc., is best handled by adding five or ten minutes to the first period of the day. Non-instructional school business should be handled at that time.

While Dr. Conant talks a great deal about twelfth-grade mathematics, I visualize comprehensive high schools in which some students will begin their studies of subjects such as calculus and physics in the tenth year of school. This is an advantage of the nongraded organization which cannot be achieved in the graded type of school organization about which Conant wrote.

The first thing that the school must do is to assess what has so far been achieved by its student body, and once their learning has been properly appraised, students should be grouped and organized into viable learning situations designed to accommodate their needs, both the imperative and the future.

In order for schools to offer programs of a broadly comprehensive nature, they must deal with an amalgamation of students. This intermingling activity pressures the high school to accomplish some sort of social fusion. From this stress comes the appellation, "truly comprehensive." This term is used to indicate broadly the intention of the school to accommodate fully and equally the needs of students of all levels of ability. The implication is that all large secondary schools must provide courses which, from the first year of high school onward, include special studies of many different kinds.

A comprehensive high school has become something which everyone knows about but very few understand. Most school administrators will define it as a school which has vocational, general, and academic education all under the same roof. Actually, the aim of the comprehensive school is to provide something educationally richer and more varied for all students.

In Great Britain the comprehensive school is unselective. It is the one school which caters to people of all levels of ability, apart from handicapped youngsters and those needing special education. In the United States, it is also unselective—but much more, it is a serious attempt to provide appropriate education, academic, vocational, or process oriented for *all* young people.

The difference between a vocational school and a comprehensive school lies chiefly in attitude and intention. The comprehensive school sets out to provide for all abilities and the vocational school attempts to educate only for a specific objective.

Let us proceed now to a more detailed, practical analysis of the Comprehensive High School. Our objective will be to draw greater meaning and value from an exciting new concept that can enrich the educational programs of high schools in all parts of the country.

B. Frank Brown

Contents

American high schools are in trouble. Taxpayers are refusing to support them, students are rebelling against them, and one group of scholars has formed an alliance aimed at eliminating them.

This chapter pinpoints the problems of secondary education and suggests a number of solutions designed to improve both the school's curricula and its public image.

A series of happenings has created a crisis of confidence in the nation's high schools. This section breaks down these happenings into six crucial areas of concern:

> The Curriculum Crisis
> The Discipline Crisis
> The Crisis in Administration
> The Crisis in Teaching and Learning
> The Crisis in Finance and Support
> The Crisis of Flight

Positive suggestions are included for resolving the critical issues affecting the schools.

As an adjunct to vocational education, most comprehensive schools offer work-study programs. In these programs students spend a part of the day at the school and another part of the school day on the job learning an occupation.

As we move into an age of leisure in which there may not be enough work to go around, the emergence of programs involving youth in service-type activities takes on increasing importance. This section is devoted to the matter of describing the nature of rescue, relief and other service, as it should exist in the comprehensive school today. Furthermore, it contains, for the first time, a complete report on the new service study programs which are emerging in the more advanced comprehensive high schools.

Youth needs service for a variety of reasons. First, they need service to obtain a better perspective of themselves and their society. Service aids in the development of self-confidence and responsibility, qualities which cannot be acquired vicariously. In essence, this exciting program provides the experience that students need as a confrontation which the schools do not currently provide.

The modern comprehensive high school must be nongraded. The nongraded organization permits unparalleled flexibility both in scheduling and programming of the curriculum. In the gradeless school organization unconventional space arrangements are allocated in the school, allowing students to work in solitude with an increasing degree of independence.

The emphasis here is on structure. Scheduling is based upon the student's level of achievement so that he can make progress on all fronts. He moves faster not only in his better classes but also in classes where his achievement level has been low.

The effect of nongrading the curriculum is to change the educational process so that students are accelerated through subject matter on a continuing rather than a yearly basis. Learning is both more appropriate and more viable when youngsters of comparable academic accomplishment and pace are grouped together.

These and other components of nongraded theory and practice are described in this section.

A comprehensive secondary school must provide a program which will meet the needs of all students. This is partly accomplished through a highly sophisticated independent study program.

This section describes the role of independent study in the comprehensive high school and a description of the expertise required for offering this kind of program.

It reports in detail about viable patterns of independent study: (1) the Educational Contract, and (2) the Enabling Notion.

The concept of independent study in the comprehensive high school is described as it relates to the new "college without walls" and the potential of independent study for bringing about corresponding "high schools without walls."

The small group as a process is being viewed with increasing interest by a growing number of professions. Psychologists, sociologists, psychiatrists and personnel managers are all adapting this technique to their professional training process. By the same token, learning in the small group is revitalizing learning in the comprehensive high school.

This chapter explores the more dynamic components of small group learning and clearly establishes it as a vital component of the new curriculum.

The issue of the new curriculum is a shift from cognitive learning to a new balance between cognitive and affective learning. The small group as a process is the technique by which this important reform is being accomplished.

7. THE VOCATIONAL PROGRAM IN THE COMPREHEN-
SIVE HIGH SCHOOL 133

Every comprehensive high school must offer, in addition to the academic program, the opportunity of a curriculum suited to the needs of minority groups. Comprehensive schools must also offer a vocational program which will provide students with the necessary skills for earning a living in one of the trades immediately after graduation. This section deals with the type of vocational program which should be provided in modern comprehensive high schools.

This chapter advances for the first time the idea of a complete vocational program contracted out to the community under the new concept of performance contracting. Vocational accountability and a broadly extended program are explained in detail.

8. THE RIGHTS AND PRIVILEGES OF STUDENTS IN THE
COMPREHENSIVE HIGH SCHOOL 149

Recent court decisions have eliminated the concept of *in loco parentis* which has been the basis for school discipline from the beginning of schools.

This section analyzes the various court decisions affecting students and the school and reports clearly on the limits of the new student freedoms.

Recommendations are made for alternative strategies for operating schools in an era in which students from kindergarten through high school have all the rights and privileges of the Bill of Rights and the Fourteenth Amendment.

9. PROS AND CONS OF THE YEAR-ROUND SCHOOL . 169

Strong revival of the concept of year-round schooling is in the making. Within recent months more schools have inaugurated year-round schooling than in the entire history of the movement, which first started around 1900.

This chapter contains a careful analysis of the new plans of year-round schooling and reports in detail the advantages and disadvantages of this reawakened movement. It contains suggestions that are important to any school, or school district, which has under advisement such a program.

This chapter contains eleven specific recommendations for transforming the conventional high school curriculum into a broadly comprehensive program of studies.

This section contains a complete reprint of the argument of the Supreme Court in the famous Tinker decision which extended the Bill of Rights and the Fourteenth Amendment freedoms to children from kindergarten through high school.

The case is important because it eliminates the concept of *in loco parentis* which has been the authority behind school discipline.

NEW DIRECTIONS
FOR THE
COMPREHENSIVE HIGH SCHOOL

1

The Comprehensive Dilemma: Sounding the Alarm

Shakespeare wrote in *Antony and Cleopatra:* "Though it be honest, it is never good to bring bad news." This sage advice is disregarded in this book. The "bad news" about the nation's high schools is so inconceivably bad that it can no longer be ignored. Paraphrasing another poet, this unfortunate institution is "on the brink of despair." It may well be that the conventional high school has so completely outlived its usefulness that it is about to sink into oblivion. If this should happen, the demise of the conventional high school, with its general education orientation, will not be a bleeding heart affair.

While this chapter appears at first glance to be a bloodletting, it is because the time has come to let blood. The conventional high school is in a serious state of intellectual disrepair and its students are the victims of "benign neglect" from their administrative and watchcare institutions, the state departments of education, and accrediting associations.

The matter is so serious and of such great concern that institutions all around the country are holding discussions on how to de-school society. For example, the Center for the Study of Democratic Institutions at Santa Barbara, California, recently held a conference on the topic, "Toward a Society Without Schools." Almost the first question raised was, "What can be done to disestablish the schools as they now exist?"

At the University of Pittsburgh a seminar called an Encounter in Education was even more to the point on how to de-school society. At this seminar, de-schooler advocate Ivan Illich suggested lawsuits against compulsory schooling. In Illich's opinion, compulsory education violates students' civil rights. In Illich's words, "An alternative to schools is not another form of schools. It is no schools."

Most of the de-schoolers are disciples of Paul Goodman, the first and most vociferous advocate of a new kind of schooling. Goodman's case for radically changing schooling is based on the fact that in the early part of this century only 6% of the population completed high school and fewer than 1% went on to college. The point is that the country was pretty well run in 1900 by school dropouts.

Anyway, the debate over whether and how to get rid of schools, especially high schools, is just beginning—more and louder voices can expect to be heard. The gist of the matter is that there are forces at work which threaten the American value that education is desirable and that everyone must have it. There is burgeoning a widening attack on the desirability of formal education.

What has caused the problem? The high school curriculum and organization have not been changed since the early part of the century. At that time there was a thorough reorganization as the result of what educators considered "suicidal specialization" and "excessive smattering." This was caused by students either specializing excessively, or smattering their efforts over a variety of subjects having no relation to one another.

In 1918, in an effort to eliminate both the specialization and smattering problems, in one fell swoop the Commission on Reorganization of Secondary Education issued its famous Cardinal Principles of Education. These functions, which became universally known as the seven principal objectives of secondary education, are as follows:

> health
> command of the fundamental processes
> worthy home membership
> a vocation
> civic education

worthy use of leisure time
ethical character

The seven Cardinal Principles and their resulting guidelines served their purpose well for half a century, but they are now hopelessly out of date. For example, the notion of building ethical character through the use of the Holy Bible was stricken down by the Supreme Court. Several of the other objectives are equally out of keeping with the times.

The root of the problem of the secondary school is that both curricula and organization are still geared to objectives established in 1918. Since that time, there has been no new national statement of high school goals, purposes, or function; yet society and its other institutions have changed radically.

THE SOCIAL REVOLUTION

Another complicating factor is the revolution of youth. The nation is currently in the throes of a social revolution involving youth which has enormous implications for change in the secondary schools. Aspects of this revolution which have direct bearing on the high schools are:

(1) The Tinker Case, in which the Supreme Court eliminated the concept of *in loco parentis* and ruled that school children have the right to express their political views all the way from kindergarten through high school.
(2) Court rulings on dress and the deportment of students with special reference to such things as long hair, beards, mini skirts, and pant suits.
(3) Changes in social action, e.g. student protests and the increase in teacher strikes.
(4) Issues of morality, particularly with reference to changing attitudes toward sex.
(5) The decline of the work ethic as one of the nation's most significant values. Nearly all labor strikes now include requests for a drastic reduction in the work week. Most demands are for a 25 to 28 hour week.
(6) The enormous acceleration in communications.
(7) The increased organization of society.

(8) The concern of black people about black people's problems and the status of integration.

(9) More recently, the growing concern of white people about white people's problems.

(10) The agitation of feminists for "equality."

(11) The rejection of a possession-oriented society by much of the new generation.

(12) The new emphasis on improving the environment.

(13) Court approval of the 18-year-old vote and the added emphasis this has given to the determination of young people to achieve greater participation in their own affairs.

The components of high school education most radically affected by the social revolution are:

(a) Interpersonal relations—the changing relationship between persons of dissimilar race, opposite sex, or different social class.

(b) Teaching and learning—since the beginning, this activity has centered around teaching and the teacher, but more recently the emphasis has shifted to learning and the student; and the big question is no longer how to teach, but how to learn.

It is difficult to assess which of these two components will have the most impact on the reformation of the curriculum. In the immediate future, the matter of interpersonal relationships will have more effect than the instructional component of teaching and learning. Causation is the changing relationship between persons of dissimilar race, opposite sex, and people of different social class.

Over the long haul it is hoped that the revolution in teaching and learning will be the more influential factor in revolutionizing the high school. After all, these happenings are the major function of the schools. Epitomized, the big question is no longer how to teach, but how to learn. So, at some point in the future one can expect far more emphasis on learning which, in the past, has been so subordinated to teaching that it has been a secondary or tertiary happening in the pleasant groves of academe.

THE COLEMAN REPORT

A mandate for change even more compelling than the social revolution is the famous Coleman Report. In a research study involving 4,000 schools, 60,000 teachers and 645,000 pupils, Professor James Coleman of Johns Hopkins University found that only about 15% of the time in school is time well spent.

The report has been heralded as a dictum for educational change and school improvement. Christopher Jencks, in an article for *The New Republic,* refers to the Coleman Report as "the most important piece of educational research in years." Others consider it to be the most significant educational study of all time. The report casts such a serious reflection on the educational establishment that it causes one to question the value of both past and present theories of teaching and learning.

Much has been said and written in the last several years about a Credibility Gap. The gap between what high schools are and what they should be is so incredible that I can only refer to it as the Incredibility Gap.

NEW GOALS

Formerly, the primary purpose of education was the development of the intellect. Unfortunately, too many high schools are continuing to function as if this were still the major goal of education.

Within the past decade the purpose of education has changed radically, and it is becoming increasingly clear that *the new goal of education is to produce individuals who are capable of making wise decisions.* If we are to achieve this goal, then the high school curriculum should minimize the required number of courses and provide students with as many electives and alternatives as possible. Unless students have experience in making choices and decisions when they are young, they will not be well prepared for making decisions in adult life.

The academic atmosphere should be loosened and variegated so that high school students may choose not only their courses, but their teachers as well. While most administrators quail at the thought of students picking and choosing their teachers, experience has shown that when privileged to select, students invariably fill up the classes of the better teachers first and force weak and incompetent teachers to do some very serious soul searching.

Unfortunately, schools have been against choices and alternatives for students, instead of being for them. Their attitudes toward student choice are reflected in one of the cartoon strips involving Peanuts:

> "I learned something in school today. . . . I signed up for folk guitar, computer programming, stained glass art, shoemaking, and a natural foods workshop. . . . I got spelling, history, arithmetic, and two study periods."
>
> "So, what did you learn?"
>
> "I learned that what you sign up for and what you get are two different things."[1]

DIVERSITY OF DEVELOPMENT

In essence, the high school curriculum should be designed for a changing world that can be rewarding and defeating, stimulating and frustrating, as well as exciting and boring almost at the same time. In order to accomplish this goal, there must be a new commitment to the concept of *diversity of development!* This notion allows wide latitude in the kind of program which different individuals will pursue in the effort to achieve varying potential. Some students will follow a rigorous academic program; others, more interested in other pursuits, will pay academe scant courtesy.

The aforementioned expression of the school's new purpose, to produce individuals who can make wise choices and good decisions, contrasts with the philosophy of more liberal educators who consider the chief function of the school to be social processing. Somewhat frustrated by the discovery and expansion of new knowledge which we have neither the time nor the energy to assimilate, this group takes the view that learning is not for all students but only for those with accentuated tastes and undisguised abilities. The rest should be concerned with major problems of society, especially equality.

---

[1] Dialogue from *Peanuts,* Charles Schultz.

It is in this setting that the comprehensive high school takes on new meaning. Diversity of program and activities continually increases as society changes. The ultimate aim is the widest possible variation of individual programs.

TOWARDS A DEFINITION

The general public which, in the past, has remained largely uncritical about its community's high schools, is beginning to assume an attitude of constructive discernment as to what should be taught and when. This new concern of parents and taxpayers is bringing about action which is being tactfully referred to as "constructive turbulence." To put it bluntly, there is a new tough-mindedness abroad in the land as to what the high schools should be about. The main concern is with the new comprehensiveness which increasing numbers of people feel should be the chief business of the high school.

In an effort to reach agreement as to what is meant by the comprehensive high school, one must first turn to James B. Conant's original definition which described the community comprehensive high school as a secondary school with programs that serve the needs of all of the youth in the community. While this statement could hardly be more nebulous, it is certainly all encompassing and describes in vague terms what the public wants and is beginning to demand from its secondary schools.

CRITERIA FOR COMPREHENSIVENESS

Even though only a modicum of change has taken place in the high schools within the last century, the principles on which the modern comprehensive secondary curriculum should be based have emerged with clarity. The basic components are as follows:

(1) Achievement grouping in the four basic subjects of English, mathematics, science, and history.
(2) A nongraded class organization which allows any student to pursue any subject in which he has an interest and is capable of handling.
(3) An adequate number of counselors to assist in matching

the student to his curriculum. The important thing is the "match."

(4) A reading laboratory for handicapped readers.
(5) A writing laboratory for students who are unable to express themselves well in writing.
(6) Speed-reading courses for sophisticated readers.
(7) College preparatory courses for students who plan to continue their education.
(8) Numerous opportunities for vocational training both at school and away from school during the school day. This program should be available for both boys and girls.
(9) A vocational program which allows the student to receive training in any established vocation through a performance contract between the school and a local training agency.
(10) Supervised work study, both semi-vocational and maturity-process types.
(11) Supervised service study programs.
(12) A school day organized into six or more periods with provisions for up to four or even five periods to be studied off campus.
(13) School programs which allow the student freedom to choose what he will study with required courses being confined to skills and basics.
(14) A program of independent study in all of the disciplines.
(15) An open campus which allows students to come and go in line with their needs and interests.

NEW PATHS TO THE DIPLOMA

One of the bigger and better breakthroughs in secondary education is the new involvement program in which a student can obtain a diploma on a job-entry plan after the tenth grade of schooling.

The job-entry plan permits 16-year-olds to leave school at the end of the tenth year and complete their diploma on the job. Any student who has ten credits and successfully demonstrates job efficiency can select this alternative to classroom training.

The plan allows him to be awarded one additional credit for each seven weeks of successful work experience and receive his diploma when he has a total of 15 credits, including the ten he earned in the classroom.

The second new pathway to a high school diploma is a "student performance program." This permits students to finish high school when they have fulfilled previously outlined means and objectives as measured by performance. Credits or lengths of time in school are not factors.

Perhaps the other significant new trend in the high school is to break up the traditional box-box classroom organization by rearranging the school into communities of learning. What schools are doing here is to take roughly four classrooms which would ordinarily house 120 students and make these a learning community. The intent here is to begin to extend the high school into the larger learning community of the surrounding city. This notion is still in its genesis and is largely a response to the movement toward free schools, of which there are now over 2,000.

The other well-established happenings in improving curricula are the increase in:

(1) Field courses in which the students are doing vastly more field work.
(2) More laboratory courses, calling for more individual involvement.
(3) The mini courses which may run anywhere from two to three days to two to three weeks. (A mini course is a course built around a single concept or value.)
(4) Work-study programs (nonvocational type) in which every student spends time on a job before graduation.

NONACADEMIC OBJECTIVES

In addition to the foregoing components, there are certain objectives of a nonacademic nature towards which the comprehensive school should be oriented. These objectives were established at an Anglo-American conference on the secondary school which was sponsored by the Ditchley Foundation at Ditchley Park, England, in 1967:

> Emotional health,
> Concern for others,

Concept for integrity,
Intellectual curiosity,
Capacity to make wise decisions,
Enjoyment of aesthetic experience,
Encouragement of creativity.

The Anglo-American conferees agreed further that a youngster learns as much from his school environment as he does in a classroom situation and that a prime objective of this school is to help him learn to live with others.

While high schools have always allowed students to drop out, they should now eliminate rigid attendance rules and allow them to "drop in" as well. Increasingly, there is a need for "occasional learning," and high schools which are really serving a community should be responsive to this need. More and more often students who are not in high school, and adults as well, should be accommodated in high schools by allowing them to take a mini course, or sit in on a seminar or forum which is of interest.

THE CURRICULUM

A major function of the high school has been to prepare students for college. The colleges and universities have grown away from the liberal arts tradition as the *sine qua non,* but the high schools continue to stress liberal arts curricula for the academically talented to the exclusion of other educational opportunities.

There are two reasons for the laggardness of schools in changing from their conventional programs to more flexible offerings:

(1) They are subject to economic reprisals if their patrons do not approve the change.
(2) Administrators generally are more interested in programs which will allow them to account for every student every minute, than in pioneering with programs which might bring new vitality to the curriculum.

It is a sad commentary on education that the changes that have been made in the curriculum have been generated neither by administrators nor by educational theorists. In the late 1950's and 1960's a vast improvement was made in subject matter, but this was accomplished by college and university scholars. By far the greatest impact was made by Jarrold Zacharias of M.I.T. who revolutionized high school physics and, in the process, developed a model for improving the other disciplines.

Having accomplished their objective of strengthening their discipline, there is nothing more that the scholars can do. They have no entry into the high school except through their particular discipline. Since the educational theorists have proved to be completely impotent and ineffective, future change in the curriculum and operation of the high school can come only from the administrator and his teaching staff.

What should the school's new curricula be like? In the past, schools have emulated one another. The result has been a national duplication of almost a single program. To look at one high school is to look at them all. The only major differences are in the exterior trappings.

The schools must now become highly individualized. They should move so rapidly to new programs that there is no time for the duplication process. For instance, enrollment in foreign language courses is down nearly 40% and other traditionally strong academic courses are losing ground. The surviving core in the curricula is language arts, mathematics, and science. These courses continue to attract nearly all students, but the rest of the formal curricula is in deep trouble.

The comprehensive curriculum for the seventies should abandon many of today's courses. It should be redeveloped around a troika of language arts, science, and mathematics, with these courses serving as the base-line program for all students. Time in the troika subjects should comprise a maximum of half of the student's day. The rest of the curriculum should revolve around field studies, mini courses, and service learning, using the community as both the classroom and the laboratory. The school should service the new off-campus learning in springboard fashion. In essence, an increasing amount of the school's program of teaching and learning which has been relegated into what has been called a school, must now take place in the larger community of the world of work and service. The function of the school is to prepare students for these activities and launch them as soon as they are ready.

While many high schools are lowering the standards of the traditional academic program because of the influx of minority groups, what they should be doing instead is inaugurating alternative programs. The new high school curricula must be so exciting that it will completely replace the old fashioned continuation schools which traditionally accommodate dropouts and adults.

It is time to recognize that most of the high school innovations of the sixties not only failed in the sixties but are also inappropriate to the seventies. Team teaching, which was widely heralded a decade ago by the Ford Foundation and the National Association of School Principals, is as dead as a doornail. Interestingly enough, although it originated as a high school innovation, high school teachers completely rejected the concept. But it has found a home in the new open plan elementary schools where it is going strong.

Modular scheduling, while not yet as passé, is rapidly disappearing from the educational scene. It is now abundantly clear that "juggling the time" in a class is of no consequence. What is important is what happens in the class.

The only innovation from the sixties which has survived as a viable notion is nongradedness. This has served to open up the curriculum. It is not only well established as a bridge between the traditional and a better way, but it has great promise as a method for giving the curriculum even more openness.

So, while the schools have suffered from the trauma of innovations which didn't work and do decidedly lament their loss of authority as the result of court decisions over dress codes and student rights, there are new and salutory ways of dealing with students. As a matter of fact, the curriculum will be much stronger when the school finally gives up its role as a fortress isolated from the community. In essence, the community will become an extension of the school and the students will go forth from the school to learn. About all that is needed is for the school to reallocate its resources and launch a triumvirate of activities involving work-study programs, service-learning activities, and field work opportunities.

The important thing about the new curriculum is that it takes into consideration some basic beliefs about learning. These are:

(1) The human potential for learning is great.
(2) Learning takes place easily and is exciting when the student perceives its relevance.
(3) The best learning is learning by doing.
(4) Learning is more lasting when the student participates responsibly in the process.

The intent, then, of the new curriculum is to develop in students a responsible commitment to involvement in the world of today which will carry over into the world of tomorrow.

THE PUBLIC'S ATTITUDE

For the past several years, George Gallup, the pollster, has conducted an *Annual Survey of the Public's Attitude Towards the Public Schools.* In the 1970 survey, the greatest concern of the public was discipline. The 1971 survey pinpointed finances as the biggest concern. Both of these issues must be taken into consideration when a high school develops alternatives to the conventional program.

What about discipline in the newly described curriculum? First, it should be stated that it is no longer possible to maintain the "sit down and be quiet" method which has prevailed since schools first came into existence. The courts have repudiated the concept of *in loco parentis* by which the teacher could act in the place of the parent. The Supreme Court in particular, has extended the Bill of Rights and the Fourteenth Amendment to all students, regardless of age.

The nub of the matter is that it is now well-nigh impossible to maintain discipline when a student is subject to six periods a day, with thirty students in each class. The very relevance of the new curriculum solves this problem. Students are responsibly involved for half of the school day in field, service, or work functions in which they have an interest. Minimizing the "cage" time of the class has a highly salubrious effect on student behavior.

With reference to cost, the new curriculum can be devised to cost much less than the existing program, as it requires fewer teachers and less expenditure for materials. The new concept, furthermore, makes extensive use of volunteers and widely uses student talents in tutorial activities. It is anything but a "public be damned" cost program. It is actually responsive to the concerns of the public, as described by Dr. Gallup.

SUMMARY

The most significant thing about the comprehensive school is its deep concern for the spread of ability among all of the students involved in its program. Before curriculum building can be begun, this must be properly analyzed on a statistical basis. The school must also carefully determine information about where its pupils have come from, their abilities, and their background, in order to plan its overall program. In general, a completely comprehensive school will contain a population highly heterogeneous in ability with a program which emphasizes their peculiar needs.

In the effort to achieve greater comprehensiveness, the schools must increasingly strive towards a new openness. We have had a heritage from our English ancestors of keeping the elite educated while depriving ourselves of potential leaders from the underprivileged. In the 70's, the schools belong to everyone, and everyone should have access to as little or as much schooling as he desires at any given time. Even the Jeffersonian statement on public schools to the effect that each year we shall rake a score of geniuses from the ashes of the masses is not sufficiently democratic for the mood of the country in the 70's.

Schools should no longer be built for one purpose, but for a wider community use. Nor should the school attempt to house all of the learning which a student must acquire. Young people must be encouraged to play an active part in the society which they, themselves, will mold.

This new concept has enormous implications for change in the school's curriculum. The community, its service-type institutions, its businesses, and its cultural agencies, must become an extension of the school and furnish the environment for intensive service opportunities, work study, and field work. The new learning environment will be diffused throughout the community and beyond. The result will be a dispersal of student learning imaginatively projected throughout the entire community.

2

The Six Crises
in the High School

When George Washington was in the White House, he sent Gouvenor Morris to France to find out what kind of a king Louis XVI was. After several months in France, envoy Morris returned and reported: "Mr. President, Louis XVI is a good king, as despots go, but he has inherited a revolution."

By the same token, when President Nixon asked his secretary of Health, Education and Welfare, Elliot Richardson, what kind of teachers and administrators were running the nation's high schools, Mr. Richardson is said to have replied: "Mr. President, they are good teachers and administrators, as teachers and administrators go, but they have inherited a revolution."

The revolution in secondary education is based upon six crises:

- The first crisis has come about as a consequence of an outdated and mediocre program of studies.
- The second is a result of the schools' inability to change their antiquated methodology.
- The third crisis is a creation of the Supreme Court caused by the abolition of the legal basis for discipline and bestowing the privileges of the Bill of Rights and the 5th and 14th Amendments on all students from kindergarten through high school.
- Crisis number four has been foisted on the schools by the teacher training institutions and the state departments of education.

- The fifth crisis has developed because of the increasing militancy on the part of teachers and students.
- The sixth crisis is an amalgamation of the first five which has resulted in the burgeoning free school movement.

During 1970 the schools came close to having a seventh crisis. This was over the issue of sex education. The turmoil over this issue subsided when the schools abandoned their plans for sex education programs after angry parent groups all across the country protested vigorously over this new encroachment on the home by the school.

It is amusing to examine the schools' argument for the case of teaching sex education focused against the facts. The schools' case rested largely on the increase in venereal disease, and their entry into the sex education field was based on the need to properly inform students and prevent this happening. The truth of the matter is that, in Sweden, there has been an elaborate sex education program in the schools for fifty years; yet the incidence of sex disease among girls has been reported as being the highest in the world.

The sad part about the sex education incident is that too often schools get themselves on a see-saw between community groups, and in this way they compound their already complex problems. In this case, the villains were the various local medical societies which encouraged the schools to undertake the development of thorough programs in sex education. The parents, especially the conservative ones, rose up to protest in great numbers and the schools became the whipping boy between various pro and con groups, with the cons winning by more than the proverbial mile. The only loser was the schools. The unfortunate part about this kind of happening is that each time the schools go through one of these exercises they come out the big loser in prestige and community support.

THE CURRICULUM CRISIS

The crisis in the curriculum is an outcome of the changing attitude of the young as a result of their having been reared in an affluent society. The affluence of their environment has allowed them to grow up without developing either any historical curiosity or any aesthetic curiosity. For example, they see no relationship between what they call their "need for awareness," and ancient or medieval history. They have no curiosity about classical music, feeling that rock is the essence of musical creation.

An outcome of the crisis in learning is the drop in applications to colleges, despite the fact that the high schools are graduating more students than ever before. Instead of going to college, many high school graduates are more interested in going to Albuquerque and taking sensitivity training, or participating in some other high involvement fad.

Another factor which contributes indirectly but significantly to the crisis in the liberal arts curriculum tradition is the development of the birth control pill and the corresponding liberalized attitude towards sex. In essence, the desire for "instant happiness" and the fad to "do one's thing" have resulted in a loss of interest in the liberal arts and the long tradition that this is the body of knowledge which is of most worth.

If the curriculum crisis is to be resolved, then there must be a new and increased understanding on the part of the student as to what he is to learn and why. For far too long teachers have kept goals and objectives to themselves, if indeed there ever were any.

The student must submit in writing, no later than the second session, what he expects to get out of the course. He must test this objective constantly in the crucible of what he is learning, and one fourth of the way, at mid point, and three quarters of the way through the course, he must evaluate in writing what he has actually learned and what he feels he should have learned. The intent is to have each student set his goals and stick with them.

Every student must read several things each week which relate to his initial goals. He must submit something in writing each week about his goals in the course. After the teacher has examined this document he should then make it available to the other students in order that the class can share what they are learning or not learning with one another. All students are requested to read the reports of their fellow students and urged to make comments about them; these comments should be channeled back to the student concerned. This is an effective technique for helping students understand the why of the curriculum and develop strategies for learning.

THE DISCIPLINE CRISIS

The crisis in discipline was brought to a head by two Supreme Court cases which resulted in a vast erosion of the authority of the school. The first of these cases was the Case of West Virginia v. Barnette Supra. In this case, Mr. Justice Jackson, in speaking for the court, said:

> The 14th Amendment . . . protects the citizen against the state, itself, and all its creatures—Boards of Education not excepted.

In essence, the court ruled that not only were students in public school not to be compelled to salute the flag, but also that they had all the freedoms of the Bill of Rights under the 14th Amendment.

The second case which further corroded the authority of schools is the case of John F. Tinker and Mary Beth Tinker, minors, v. Des Moines Independent Community School District.

In this case, Mr. Justice Fortas delivered the opinion of the court, of which the following is an excerpt:

> First Amendment rights, applied in light of the special characteristics of the school environment, are available to teachers and students. It can hardly be argued that either students or teachers shed their constitutional rights to freedom of speech or expression at the schoolhouse gate.

The effect of these two cases has been to destroy the concept of *in loco parentis* in which teachers had the same authority for discipline as the parents when children were under their supervision. By making students in school "persons under the constitution," the courts have indeed deprived the schools of the legal basis for their authority. Since the beginning the schools have been authoritarian institutions and they have been unable to develop alternate strategies to their commitment to authority for managing hundreds of students located in one building.

In the crisis of discipline, history is repeating itself. The progressive education movement of the thirties failed because of the emphasis on freedom of movement and the resulting lack of discipline which parents referred to as "the chaos in the schools." The principles of progressive education, which involved a voluntary abolition of authority by the teachers, have, in effect, now been made compulsory by the United States Supreme Court. So, the Court decisions through bestowing constitutional freedoms on students have had the effect of mandating a new kind of progressive education.

Whether the schools will be successful in developing alternate strategies for managing their charges is yet to be seen. What *is* clear is that many high school students lack the maturity of self-discipline which is so necessary in a permissive atmosphere. The failure to resolve this dichotomy makes for a continuing crisis.

THE CRISIS IN ADMINISTRATION

The crisis in school administration has been fomenting for a long time. This crisis has its roots in the selection and training of teachers for the job of administration.

Originally, the word principal referred to the principal or head teacher in the school, and the principal teacher, who was usually the most outstanding teacher on the staff, functioned as the school's head. Later, the teacher training institutions got into the act and with the collaboration of their fellow educators in the state department of education, rules for the certification of principals were established. These rules grew until they now require the completion of a whole host of courses built around boring and inappropriate educational theory. It is no wonder that the science of education, if there is such a thing, is becoming widely known as "the dismal science."

What happened, as the number of courses for certification in administration grew in number and ennui, was that many of the more scholarly and able teachers rebelled against the tiresome exercise of putting in a years' work on educational matter which they considered to be a gross waste of time. Consequently, some

of the more able members of the teaching staff have become in-
eligible for the principalship. Almost equal in criticism to the
poor quality of professional education are complaints about the
lack of quality among the staff of teacher training institutions
which teach these courses. They are widely referred to as "timid
and obsolete people."

The gist of the matter is that rigid certification rules eliminate
many able and talented teachers from consideration for principal-
ships.

A major pool for the principalship, in the past, has been the
athletic coach. His training and ability to discipline have served
the schools well in the past but, since by order of the Supreme
Court, the schools can no longer operate under the concept of
authoritarianism which was developed by the coach-breed, then
it is strongly recommended that the Master's degree in Administration and Supervision be abolished as a requirement for the
principalship. This will allow able teachers who have a Master's
degree in their discipline to serve in the principalship. These individuals, with their scholarly background, comprise a more capable
pool of potential administrators. Their achievement in their own
discipline qualifies them to head up an institution engaged in the
business of teaching and learning. These individuals have a much
greater potential for developing new strategies for managing and
directing high school learning than the present limited source.
This is not heresy; there are no certification rules for the college
presidency, then why should there be any for the principalship?

Another significant part of this problem is that, under the philosophy of authoritarianism and ironclad discipline, school boards
concentrated on the employment of men as administrators. School
boards have long labored under the false assumption that men are
stronger disciplinarians than women. Women should now be considered equally with men for administrative posts. With the opening up of the selection process to include capable women career
teachers, the source of administrators will be broadened enormously.

Actually, the best teachers in the schools are women anyway.
This is accounted for by the fact that industry has always discriminated against women and all of the professions have been in
competition for the brightest and most able men while education

has been the only field that aggressively recruits women. Industry, of course, has been far more successful in the competition for bright and able men because of higher salaries and greater chance for promotion. When Francis Keppel was Dean of the graduate school of education at Harvard, studies under his direction clearly demonstrated that because of this happening the best market for teachers was women. It is past time to consider them equally for the principalship and other top administrative jobs.

The numerous confrontations between administrators and teachers on the one hand, and administrators and students on the other, have made it abundantly clear that school administration must now change. The first step calls for a widening of participation by both students and teachers in the administrative decision-making process. The second step requires an opening up of narrow certification rules, so that the person best qualified is eligible for the principalship, and not just the person with the most courses in administration and supervision.

THE CRISIS IN TEACHING AND LEARNING

The inability of the teacher to focus on learning instead of teaching has aroused universal concern over the effectiveness of the high school. Perhaps Socrates prognosticated the role of the teacher better than anyone else when he compared the teacher to the midwife. In the Socratic philosophy the teacher's job is to deliver learning. Instead of delivering learning, the teacher has been delivering teaching. There is a vast difference between teaching and learning and for too long teachers have equated these functions.

Perhaps Charlie Keller, former professor of Williams College and erstwhile director of the John Hay Fellows program, epitomized this crisis better than anyone else when he commented, "Too many teachers use the cover all approach when the important thing is not what to cover, but what to cut out."

The nub of this crisis is that there has been a far greater emphasis on teaching than on learning. In classrooms throughout the length and breadth of the land, teachers talk endlessly, hour after monotonous hour. The result is that teaching is a passive exercise with too little involvement of the learner. This crisis can be resolved only if there is a major shift of emphasis from teaching to learning.

A number of attempts have been made to accomplish this happening, but none of them has had wide success. The team teaching movement of the sixties with millions of dollars of support from the Ford Foundation was the most significant effort to change the imbalance in teaching and learning. Unfortunately, instead of lessening the emphasis on teaching, team teaching actually increased it, with the result that the movement failed as a high school innovation.

The problem with team teaching at the high school level was this: When Lloyd Trump, the chief architect of team teaching, first described it, he suggested that students spend 40% of their time in large groups (one hundred or more), viewing and listening or being taught by a master teacher; 40% of their time in independent study; and 20% of their time in small groups of from 12 to 15 students. Actually, Dr. Trump suggested this division only as a guideline, but the early literature on team teaching did not explain this and this division of time was taken by the teachers as gospel. Furthermore, the pedagogy even in the guidelines was so soft that it was contributory to the failure of the program. For example, high school students should never spend 40% of their time in passive listening situations; furthermore the recommendations of from 12 to 15 for a discussion group is far too many for a small group learning situation. Eight is the maximum number of individuals who can communicate effectively in a small group. (This analysis is not intended to denigrate the work of Trump who has done more than anyone else to stir principals into action to improve schools.)

The resolution of the crisis in teaching and learning can happen only if the schools operate on a four-day week with teachers having one day of each week for the planning of learning. The process by which one brings about learning calls for far more planning and work than does the process of teaching. I strongly recommend a four-day week for teachers, with Wonderful Wednesday a day for students to be out of school in service-learning or work-study activities. This will result in immediate and drastic improvement in the schools and will not cost any more money.

In fact, it will save money on electrical, heating, and water bills. These items come to a considerable amount in high schools.

THE CRISIS IN FINANCIAL SUPPORT

The fifth great crisis is one of finance, as taxpayers everywhere revolt against the paying of school taxes. This attitude on the part of taxpayers has been fostered by two happenings: (1) teacher militancy often resulting in strikes; and (2) student activism.

The response is often made that taxpayers are not revolting just against the high schools, but against all schools. When the facts are examined closely, it is clear that while they are indeed revolting against paying taxes for any school, the precipitating irritation comes from the high schools. High school teachers are far more militant than elementary school teachers and student activism in the public schools has been concentrated almost entirely in the high schools.

With reference to the resolution of this crisis, the National Education Association, the largest of the teacher unions, seems to be aware of the need for adopting a more moderate attitude. Teacher militancy has lost for teachers much more than it has gained. Militant demands reached their cresting point in Florida in 1968 when the NEA and its Florida affiliate called a statewide teachers' strike against the Florida legislature. When the governor failed to be badgered into calling the legislature into session the effort failed miserably, and there has been no statewide strike since the Florida debacle.

The fact that thousands of teachers lost six weeks' pay, tenure, and many even their jobs has had a very sobering effect on the militant leaders of the NEA. This was the most disastrous strike in the history of teacher militancy and three years later the National Education affiliate, the Florida Education Association, is still licking its wounds and trying to rebuild to its pre-strike membership.

In many ways the NEA leadership has been more moderate of late, and this change in policy seems to be adding to the prestige and status which the organization has always enjoyed as the largest teacher professional organization.

With reference to student activism, there needs to be a new understanding between the schools and their students as to the responsibility of the student, how he expresses his freedom, and what is proper dissent. Until this happening takes place, there will continue to be trouble with students.

One of the unfair and illegal practices in most high schools is the matter of requiring a C average or better before a student can become a cheerleader, run for an office, or join a service club. If, as the Supreme Court has ruled, "students in school are persons under the Constitution," then any student should be allowed to run for any office or join any club, with the exception of the school's honor society. Some spokesmen for student's rights, such as School Superintendent Thomas Shaheen of San Francisco, even question the legitimacy of requiring a grade average for admission to the honor society. Superintendent Shaheen calls for the abolition of high school honor societies. I disagree strongly with the Shaheen doctrine and feel that recognition of superb achievement is a legitimate business of the school.

In essence, if the school is to have the support of its student consumers, and it must have, then it must find more effective ways of dealing with them and in the process eliminate all school rules which may be unfair, or are continuing points of dissension. If it is to have the support of its community and taxpayers, then there must be visible a good relationship between the school and its students.

THE CRISIS OF FLIGHT

The high schools have always had a flight problem as students fled from the school into the job market. The opening of Free Schools has given dissatisfied students a new place to flee to, and the flight from the conventional high schools is increasing at an alarming rate.

Unless the schools resolve their differences with their students, the trend toward disestablishment of schooling and Free Schools will continue to grow. The Free School movement has already become so extensive that an examination of its status and role is pertinent to the crises confronting the public high schools. The inclination of many students to enter a free school is perpetuating the sixth and perhaps the greatest crisis for the public schools. It is an amalgamation of the other five crises.

A RADICAL ALTERNATIVE—FREE SCHOOLS

Only three or four years ago schools were establishment places where practically everybody thought all young people belonged. More recently, increasing numbers of students have found the ritual of compulsory schooling not at all to their liking. What is the alternative? The only option which has emerged with vigor is the Free School. The Free School movement, catering to disenchanted students and staffed by dissident teachers and other alienated groups, is changing the notion that all young people should be in a conventional high school.

While college students' activism was energized by the Vietnam War and the issue of Civil Rights, high school activists have been more concerned with freedom and students' rights. By freedom, high school students mean power over their own destiny, and by student rights, they refer to making decisions about the organization of the school, the curricula, who teaches them, and what they are taught.

Since most of the "establishment" high schools have resisted both the demand for freedom and the clamor for students' rights, advocates of the Free School movement consider the high schools inhuman and monolithic.

Parents and teachers who are supportive of student freedom have assisted in the setting up of Free Schools. In fact, the movement is so widespread that there were reported to be roughly 2,000 Free Schools in the U.S. in 1971. Among the leading Free Schools are the Parkway School in Philadelphia; the Berkeley Free School in Berkeley, California; the Mary Road School in Newton, Massachusetts; and the Metro High School in Chicago. More often than not the Free School is opened in a vacant store; none of them have the niceties or affluence of establishment schools.

The preferred model of the Free Schools is a separate function from the public schools staffed and operated by a strong but estranged parent group, disaffected teachers, and volunteers from one, or several, local organizations. Teachers range from "dropout" public school teachers working for base subsistence, to college students volunteering their time.

In contrast to the structured and restrained attitude which establishment schools have towards their students, the disposition of the staff of the Free School is one of total permissiveness. Free Schools are extremely democratic and nonauthoritarian. Politically, Free Schools are doctrinaire with inclinations toward radical politics, usually the far left.

The prototype for Free Schools is A. S. Neil's Summerhill School in England. The theories which Neil advanced in his book *Summerhill* serve as the intellectual basis for the philosophy, curriculum, and operation of the Free School.

There are a few Free Schools which are housed in the same building as a public school, but on an after-hours basis. This is usually an alternative provided by a school system to keep from changing existing high schools. The operation of a Free School by a public school system reduces the pressure for change on the public schools.

The program of studies of Free Schools takes into account the Three R's but the big emphasis is on self-concept and personal growth and understanding. Almost equal stress is put on overcoming barriers which separate schools from the community.

The word "free" means much more than merely student freedom. It connotes that every Free School is free to do its own thing. The result is a wide variation in programs among Free Schools.

One of the great difficulties facing the Free Schools is the low regard which the public has for them. In addition to the lack of public and professional acceptance, most state departments of education refuse to certify their teachers. There are also obvious pressures against them from public school teachers and administrators.

In spite of these disadvantages, many educational sources feel that Free Schools may signal new directions in education, especially for education within the big cities. Certainly there is a need for alternatives to the conventional high school. The Free School is a decidedly different kind of school and a radical alternative to the traditional establishment school.

Undoubtedly, the first and most vociferous critic of the conventional schools was Paul Goodman. It was he who pointed out so effectively that the schooling experiences have undergone a radical change within the last seventy years.

Goodman has been joined, and at times outranked, in the quantity of school criticism by Ivan Illich, John Holt, and Jonathan Kozol. What these school critics object to most is authoritarian discipline, boredom, the overemphasis on grades, the lack of learning, and the suppression of curiosity.

The revolt against the schools is no longer a complaint about outdated curricula and mediocre teaching. It has reached such a crescendo that it is aimed at the complete disestablishment of formal schooling.

FREE SCHOOLS: TOWARD A DEFINITION

The best definition of Free Schools is found in the New Schools Exchange newsletter which recently garnered definitions from Free Schools all across the country. The definitions are a veritable plethora of potpourri. But they have great significance in their insight into what many students want their schools to be like. These inciteful comments are as follows:[2]

> A Free School is a community of people of various ages, experiences, and beliefs but with a common philosophy of people, life, and education gathered together in various groupings, at various times in various places, for the common purpose of living, experiencing, and changing (learning).
>
> Gerard F. MacMillan
> Science Educ. Center
> Univ. of Iowa
> Iowa City, IA 52240

> A free school implies a "you are essentially God-like beautiful." It is a place where we can all be free to feel out . . . who we are, and how we fit into this fantastic world. It is an extended family, multi-aged-ranged, relishing the ecstatic at-

---

[2] New Schools Exchange, 301 E. Canon Perdido, Santa Barbara, Calif. Issue Number 60, p. 5.

traction-desire to discover the ways of this world and of ourselves. It is perhaps impossible.

> Penny Harma,
> Laurence, Kansas

A free school is a place where kids of all ages and sizes jump out of the bus and burst in the door (this is a free day school) yelling "hooray!" and they drop their lunches anywhere and drop their coats on the floor, or else keep them on all day and immediately start their play or work whether or not the teachers are there yet. . . . .

> Diane Cabarga
> Monmouth Modern Day School
> 24 Union Hill Rd.
> Morgantown, N.J. 07751

A free school is growth and life, not dormancy and death, and as such reflects love, not hate.

> Bruce Luske
> 372, Apt. 2 Harold St.
> N. Plainfield, N.J. 07060

A free school is not a school. It is an attitude of an individual or group to pursue that which interests them. It is not an institution, but rather a noncompulsory environment. Filled with a growing concern for mankind through self-revelation.

> Bill Brokaw

A free school is a good place to make love—with all persons' paces fully flowering—the slow, the bizarre, the shin kickers—all consenting, when they want, without coercion, or seduction, or subterfuge—within the context of each person's most authentic level of glorious growth. . . . . . .

> Greenway & Rasberry
> Freestone (Sebastopol)
> California 95472

A free school is a way of learning yourself into the possibilities of other learning. It is personally systematized and includes all those who make themselves available in a shared enterprise. Its organizational life is at the service of its human associations.

Hal Lenke
Box 143
Clifton Forge, Va. 24422

I prefer the term organic schools. Organic implies a unity; the recognition that learning cannot be distinct from the living of one's life is both the point of coherence of the new, organic schools and the point of departure from authoritarian schools.

Brian Neilson
809 Spring Drive.
Mill Valley, Ca. 94941

Free School: a nonpublic, nonelite, nondenominational school.

Francis Wardle
DaNahazli School
Box 1806
Taos, N.M. 87571

We define a Free School as one where the students are offered meaningful choices and alternatives with regard to curriculum and attendance and have a choice in governing themselves in an environment free of competition.

Gladys Falken
1778 S. Holt Ave.
LA, CA 90035

3

Service Study Programs in the Comprehensive High School

For at least a decade, proponents of curriculum reform in the high school have talked about involving students in "service learning" activities. Unfortunately, this bright, promising heresy has not gotten past the talking stage. The dilemma is that none of the advocates of service learning have defined in lean and lucid prose what the concept means. At the risk of being accused of "dropping the other shoe," this chapter reduces the definition of service learning to the postage stamp level by energizing a succinct and easily understood definition of this elusive but viable notion. Epitomized, service learning means *learning while performing a service*. The intent is to provide high school students with the experience of performing a service for others. The proposition of service learning has always been a good one, but it is becoming more appropriate day by day.

His Royal Highness the Duke of Edinburgh, who has long advocated service as an important scheme in Great Britain, summarized the implications of service learning more effectively than anyone else when he commented:

> There is no quicker way to develop a sense of responsibility than to offer young people the chance to undertake a responsible duty and to combine this with some activity which

demands careful training and experience, skill and endur-
ance.[3]

The problem is that up to now the idea of student involvement
in service has been expostulated upon for the wrong reason and
only in broad generalities. The original concept of service learning
was based upon a concern to prepare young people for an age of
leisure time. The shortening of the work week and the deterioration
of the work ethic were the twin propelling factors. The idea of
service was considered the best means of keeping people constructively occupied. It has lately become apparent that service
learning is far more than just a vehicle to keep young people
constructively occupied. When the excitement of service learning
is focused against the desiccation of traditional classroom learning,
it becomes a vital component of the viable concept of increased
field work. Its adult carry-over value is tremendous.

SERVICE IN BRITAIN

Kurt Hahn, headmaster of Gordunston and one of the leading
exponents of service learning, feels that the big impediment to
widespread adoption of service programs is the unwillingness of
adults to relinquish responsibilities to the care of young people.
Hahn once said to me: "We must set up an accelerating ma-
chinery. In England, it takes thirty years to translate a truth into
a reality. I am an old man and cannot wait thirty years."

The British are far ahead of the United States in the development of opportunities for youth service. A National Youth Service
was established in 1939 by the then national president of the
Board of Education. This was followed by an act in 1946 which
proclaimed that Youth Service "was not to be regarded as simply
a wartime expedient, but that it should take its place as an integral
part of the national system of education." Wide powers were
written into the 1946 Act to authorize this happening.

The British program received another boost in 1958 when
the Minister of Education appointed a committee to determine the
contribution which young people might play in the life of the

---

[3] H.R.H. The Duke of Edinburgh, K.G., at the Convention on Accident Prevention
and Life-Saving, 14th May, 1963.

community and to advise what kind of financial support was needed from Parliament. They concluded, incidentally, that properly nourished opportunities are profoundly worthwhile and of special importance in a rapidly changing society.

Young people have lacked a mood of resolve and often suffer from a feeling of personal insignificance. They have a lower capacity for dealing with problems because of their lack of experience with tension and stress. Service learning provides a vehicle by which young people can acquire significant feelings of their worth and value.

Increasingly, we must break down the role of prejudice against involving young people in service activities. There is no doubt at all about the tremendous appeal of service for young people. What is needed is a massive effort to change the attitude of adults about their involvement.

Former President James Garfield inadvertently prognosticated the service problem when he said, "We may divide the whole struggle of the human race into two chapters: first, the fight to get leisure; second, what shall we do with our leisure when we get it?" The matter of shorter working hours and increased leisure time has profound implications for service activities.

The economy is rapidly moving from a manufacturing to a service economy. We must switch over to a service-type life where performing a service is as important as producing goods. A major propelling factor is the unanswered question: "Who profits the most? People who receive service or people who give it?" The evidence so far is on the side of the person performing the service.

The British approach to the problem of service is to lump Rescue, Relief, and Service together and treat them as a whole. While the emphasis in the United States is all on the notion of service as a separate component, the British program of a troika including Rescue, Relief, and Service is worth a closer look:

RESCUE in its simplest context is removal of persons in difficulty from a hostile environment to a safe one. This function needs specific and extensive training.

RELIEF implies the application of special knowledge to assist and comfort those suffering from injury, distress, or hardship as a result of exposure to an adverse environment or situation. Frequently, it may be needed before or after rescue. It, too, demands a high degree of training and experience.

SERVICE, on the other hand, can be given by those adapted adequately to their normal environment to the less fortunate and does not necessarily demand specific training.

In all three, however, there is a common purpose of good will and the alleviation of suffering. For each, some basic knowledge of first aid and an understanding of human problems are essential.

SERVICE IN THE UNITED STATES

We can put on a postage stamp what is being done in the United States about the important matter of training young people for Rescue, Relief, and Service.

Most high schools in the United States have numerous so-called service clubs. Unfortunately, the kind of service that is being performed in these clubs is lacking in vitality. This may be because the high school service clubs are emulating their more sedate parent organizations which were designed to serve another era. Among the service clubs which are found in most high schools are:

The Key Club, a junior Kiwanis Club;
The Interact Club, a boys' Rotary Club;
The Junior Civitan, a high school version of the Civitan Club;
The Junior Exchange Club.

These male clubs have their counterpart service clubs for girls, but all of them are separated by sex. This separation is undoubtedly a spin-off from the fraternity-sorority notion which has plagued our colleges and universities for over a century.

While all of these youth organizations are referred to as service clubs, their concept of service means selling fruitcakes at Christmas time and giving the proceeds to the Crippled Children's Clinic. They hardly ever tackle anything more profound. There is no emotional involvement in their projects and they are seriously in need of an "agonizing reappraisal."

The secondary schools in the U.S. are lacking in the development of a viable concept of service as it is now emerging. By service, I mean much more than merely being of assistance to someone. I am including the dimension that service comprises a broadening and tantalizing experience for the person who performs the activity.

There are, however, a few burgeoning trends towards a more action-oriented type of service in the form of young people's organizations which perform voluntary health and medical care work in hospitals. These organizations have taken two forms. First are the para-medics, a service-oriented organization for young people anticipating a career in the health or medical field, who are called "volunteers" and work directly with hospital patients as nurses' aides. Secondly, there are the Candy Stripers, an organization of girls who work in hospitals but have no contact with patients. Their area of operation is to provide support activities which do not require contact with patients. They take over such tasks as operating snack bars and arranging flowers.

PROPOSED NEW PROGRAMS

It is incumbent on the schools to widen their horizons and accept training of high school youth which happens outside of the high school building itself. Students should spend a decreasing amount of time at the school plant and have an increasing involvement in community service.

Widening of school programs means the addition of a vast amount of field work in all of the disciplines. In essence, if young people are going to vote at the age of 18, they must be encouraged to play an earlier and more active part in the society which they are responsible for developing and maintaining.

The most compelling need confronting the high school curriculum is the urgency for establishing service-learning programs. These call for a radical departure from the traditional high school service club approach. They recognize youth as part of the community and establish their importance to society. In a service-learning program designed to meet the needs of youth as individuals, there should be no hard and fast rules as to the type of service which a student performs. The activity should be highly individualized and the only restriction should be that the activity be of service in some observable way to an individual, agency, institution, or community.

Today over 80 percent of the young people stay on in school beyond the legal leaving age, which in most states is 16. When they do go out to work, they have many times the spending power which their parents had at their age. They have more physical maturity, they are inclined to marry at a younger age, and generally they accept responsibility at an earlier age. These factors comprise the justification for lowering the voting age to 18. They also warrant a loosening and variegation of high school curricula to include a vast amount of field work. The best opportunity for increased field work is in the service-learning area.

The problem with youth service programs as they have operated in the past is twofold:

(1) They have been custodial and largely the result of administrative depotism.

(2) Adults have refused to accept young people as volunteers on an equal basis.

Perhaps the greatest polarization in the high schools is the way they are locked in on requiring student attendance five days a week and from six to seven hours a day. This is an anachronism when focused against the fact that after students leave high school, many of them enter college almost immediately, and there they have unlimited freedom. They suddenly and traumatically are out from under the control of their parents, and the colleges only require them to attend classes two or three days a week.

One of the things most needed by youth is a transition from close supervision and hourly accountability to no supervision and very little accountability. This can be easily effected in the service-learning program. In this type of arrangement some students attend high school three days a week and participate in service-learning activities two days. For example, a student takes his basic high school subjects three days a week instead of the traditional five and is at school only on Mondays, Wednesdays, and Fridays. On Tuesdays and Thursdays he is involved in a service-learning situation somewhere in the community. A variation of this plan is for students to attend classes at school four days a week and report for service activity on Wonderful Wednesday.

The types of service-learning experiences available in a particular school vary with the kinds of opportunities which are available in the school's community. While some schools have dozens of possibilities for their students to become involved in, others have only a few. But almost every school in the country has access to the basic six. These are: senior citizen service, ecological service, hospital service, voter service, mental health service, and tutorial service. Since these six basic service-learning activities have broad applicability, they are treated in considerable depth.

Youth and the Senior Citizen

The rapid growth of nursing homes catering to senior citizens has created a multitude of service opportunities and a multiplicity of new demands for volunteers. While nursing facilities have burgeoned under expanding medicare programs, medicare does not begin to provide senior citizens with the kind of attention which they need, warrant, and deserve. School programs providing service-learning opportunities more effectively fill this gap than do other programs.

What are the kinds of activities available for youthful service in institutions housing the elderly?

1. Performing receptionist and hosting functions.
2. Engaging in conversation, and showing interest in problems of the elderly.
3. Pushing wheelchairs and giving the non-ambulatory a broader environment.
4. Managing portable libraries and pushing portable carts containing interesting books into rooms and to the bedside of bedridden patients.
5. Helping in the selection of reading materials.
6. Planning and arranging entertainment such as group singing.
7. Playing cards and games with the elderly. Often the aged have poor eyesight, but there is available an increasing number of games and cards with oversized figures and symbols.

Another approach is to assign high school students to specific individuals for regular visiting, after giving them a seminar on aging.

Ecology Service

Community service in the field of ecology is more complicated than the other services. Entry into this service function should be preceded by a two-week mini course involving the issues and procedures.

The first requirement in this course is a careful reading of the restrictions in federal legislation, especially the national safety standards for air and water. The techniques of small group learning should be used to make certain that both teams and individuals have good knowledge of the legislation.

After this, individuals and teams should survey the community in search of violations or noncompliances. Easy-to-operate water testing kits are available for under $300 and should be furnished by the school's science department.

Violations and noncompliances to standards should be reported to the nearest Environmental Enforcement Agency. Students' reports should be carefully documented, showing observations, tests, times, and dates.

Service in the field of ecology is a balance involving class discussion, research, and field work, with field work comprising the major involvement of the students' time.

Hospital Service

One of the services which has great appeal for some youth is volunteer work in hospitals. An obstacle to this development has been the medical profession which has failed to accept and appreciate the potential which young people have as volunteers in the field of medicine. The success of the Candy Stripers, a teenage female auxiliary to the hospital guild, is a good model for hospital service. This group has helped to break down the barrier.

Activities performed in hospital service include the following:

(1) Collecting, arranging and distributing flowers for those not fortunate enough to have some sent.
(2) Delivering flowers to patients' rooms and subsequently caring for the flowers.
(3) Visiting with patients who either are isolated from friends or relatives or seldom receive visitors.

(4) Manning a cheer cart which contains magazines, books, cosmetics, lotions and creams.
(5) Serving as floor hosts or hostesses.
(6) Working in the hospitality shop selling snacks or gifts.
(7) Manning the information desk.
(8) Manning the telephone switchboard.
(9) Serving as nurses' aides.
(10) Writing letters for orthopedically disabled patients or patients who are otherwise incapable of writing.
(11) Filling water pitchers.
(12) Transporting patients to X-ray and shower rooms.
(13) Babysitting with young children while their parents are visiting.
(14) Running errands for patients.

Voter Service

Service-learning activity involving voter registration by high school students is in no way related to the registration of minority groups. The registration of minority groups for the purpose of changing a particular political entity is completely outside the purview of the secondary school service-learning program.

A high school student engaged in service learning can, however, be helpful to all people in the voter service component of Service Study. This function is designed to remind new people to a community and new voters coming of age of registration deadlines. This can be accomplished either by telephone or letter, but the former is preferable, as new people or new voters frequently have questions to ask.

The intent of this program is to: (1) perform a service to individuals; (2) assist in strengthening democracy; (3) give young people experience in communications; (4) make participating students more acutely aware of the nuances of politics; (5) give students increased insight into the importance of the individual voter.

Service to Mental Health

The rap session in which young people with home and family problems are given a chance to talk about their problems has a growing need for participation by young people who get along well at home. Frequent participation is also needed by young people who have problems similar to those of the rappers.

Many mental health clinics are establishing rap houses and are in need of participation from both of the aforementioned groups. An increasing number of junior high schools are establishing rap classes and these are in great need of service assistance from high school students.

Tutorial Service

An important theme in the service-learning concept is the tutorial. More than any other service-learning component, the tutorial is emerging in depth. This component is wide ranging and consists of older students tutoring younger students, peers tutoring their counterparts, or even younger students tutoring older students.

The tutorial is the only activity under service learning which has any kind of history. The other components are just burgeoning. Historically, the model of students tutoring students is found in the Monitorial System which was first developed and widely used in the eighteenth century. Called the Lancasterian Monitorial System, the monitorial as a kind of tutorial was developed simultaneously by Joseph Lancaster, a Quaker, and Andrew Bell, an Anglican. The underlying principal of the eighteenth century model of monitoring was to use older students as monitors, or helpers, for the teacher. Under this procedure, the teacher instructed student monitors in a lesson and each monitor subsequently "taught the lesson" to ten or twelve younger children. The effects of the Monitorial System was to make a minimum amount of education available to larger numbers of children through the use of group methods, efficiency, and economy.

The gist of the matter is that the notion of children teaching other children is by no means a new one. Furthermore, children universally have always helped one another with their homework, both inside and outside of school. The modern tutorial as a scheme of teaching and learning differs from its historical antecedent in that its strategy is for each one to teach one, while the earlier plan of monitorial teaching and learning required each one to teach ten.

What is new in the "revival of the tutorial" are the emerging nuances of the significance of older students tutoring younger students. Perhaps the most surprising of these burgeoning subtleties is the identification of benefits which accrue to the tutor. It now appears that the tutor benefits at least equally as much as, and possibly much more than, the tutored.

Professor Herbert Thelen of the University of Chicago puts it this way,

> The University became interested in tutoring first graders (six-year olds) as a way to help fifth grade problem pupils in slum schools. We felt that discussion among the tutors about their own teaching experiences would be as valuable as the experience of tutoring.

While, out of concern for the tutee, I do not espouse this "tutor reversal concept," it is indicative of the value which accrues to the tutor.

Additional data on the value which the tutor derives from the tutorial is found in the British infant school model. During World War II, teachers in infant schools often found themselves in air-raid shelters with a group of children ranging from four to seven years of age. Frequently, these teachers were responsible for large groups of such children for considerable periods of time. Confronted with a mixed bag, they found that a lot of the mothering which was necessary under these circumstances was done quite naturally by the older children and that this was a maturing factor for these youngsters. It is from this source that the major principles upon which the British concept of Family Grouping and the Integrated Day are based.

The rapidly growing tutorial movement is taking a variety of forms, many of them quite innovative. The important thing is that both the tutor and the tutee seem to look at learning differently when it is taken out of the traditional classroom perspective. What is surprising is that the educational psychologists never discovered that a simple thing like narrowing the generation gap could have enormous impact on the process of teaching and learning.

Tutorial Models

The most widely used service tutorial model is the one where high school students go to elementary schools for the purpose of tutoring younger children several times a week. The elementary school tutee may be a slow child having difficulty or a bright child ready to move ahead. More often than not, he is one of the more capable students, as most teachers have the misguided notion that it requires an expert to work with slower children and they reserve these students for their own teaching. Actually, the slower children profit at least as much if not more than the more capable students. There is a freshness about tutorials which fascinates children. Furthermore, learning becomes much more personal.

The important thing about the service tutorial is for the teacher not to try to use the tutor as an aide, but let him do his own tutoring in his own way.

THE HIGH SCHOOL CLASS MODEL

A unique type of tutorial service is the emerging high school class model. This model has such enormous potential that it is reported in considerable depth. Under the high school model, one or more junior high schools in the same attendance area as the high school select 25 students who are assigned to the high school. Preferably, the junior high school group which is chosen are older students who do not learn easily and have been held back and required to repeat one or two grades because of failure to achieve. This tutorial plan relieves the junior high school of a group of older, highly frustrated students and lessens the need for middle schools.

These 25 students from the junior high school are assigned to a high school teacher who is also assigned 25 highly motivated high school students for each of her teaching periods. The high school students act as tutors for the junior high school students. The high school assignees represent different disciplines each period of the day. For example, period one consists of high aptitude math students; period two, able language arts students; period three, capable history students; and period four, talented science students.

The student tutors may or may not be interested in teaching as a career. The main criteria are that they have a proven record of accomplishment, are motivated towards learning, and like people. Students with these characteristics fit naturally into the system of microcosmic teaching and learning.

The Materials Problem

Admittedly, tutorial programs involving students have not all been successful. Usually this is caused by the fact that the student tutor has been required to put the tutee through remedial materials prescribed by the teacher. These materials inhibit the development of enthusiasm or spontaneity in either the tutor or the tutee. The student tutor should be allowed considerable freedom in the selection of materials and should teach from materials which he himself has planned and developed. When this happens, a measure of success is guaranteed, as the participants establish both better rapport and more enthusiasm.

The Routine

Session 1: Each period, high school tutors of a particular subject meet with the teacher (master tutor) who describes the project in broad terms and answers questions.

Session 2: The master tutor conducts a colloquium for the tutors on the project and its implications. At the colloquium, she sets the stage for small group discussions on learning.

Session 3: Tutors work in small groups with the topic "How You Learn." (The master tutor emphasizes the importance of self-learning and cautions against over-teaching.) At the end of Session 3, the teacher gives out tutorial assignments; these include tutee profiles which describe the tutee as a learner, and diagnose how much he has learned to date.

Session 4: Tutors in small groups discuss *what* and *how* they plan to teach. (The teacher master tutor roves from group to group assessing tutor insight.)

Session 5: Tutees are brought in and the tutorial begins. As the tutorial progresses, one-half of the tutors meet in small groups about every fifth or sixth session to share problems and evaluate the teaching and learning of their particular situation. These group sessions consist of a maximum of three tutors to a group. When half of the tutors are working in this arrangement, the other half of the tutors supervise the work of the tutees of the absent tutors, in addition to their own. The next day, the situation is reversed and the other half meet in small groups.

The Tutor

The tutor should realize at the outset that he is not a teacher. Tutees who are behind in learning have, in most cases, been overtaught. They do not need more of the same. With this in mind, the function of the tutor lies somewhere between the austerity of teaching and the warmth of self-learning. The tutor should use the big brother approach, and if he does this properly, he will always respond humanely. It should be clear to the tutor that he is a therapist and that criticism of the tutee must be rare and thoughtful. He should be careful never to upset the tutee, for what he really wants to accomplish is to get the tutee interested in learning for the sake of learning.

Evaluation

The program should be constantly under evaluation in order that both the tutor and tutee can be aware of the progress that is being made. This evaluation should take two forms: (1) the student tutor and the master tutor should meet frequently to evaluate the individual tutee's progress; (2) the master tutor should administer standardized tests quarterly. This strategy not only provides an objective evaluation of progress but it also furnishes information for continued diagnosis and prescription.

The Oblique

After a period of time, if it becomes apparent that a student is not learning from his tutor a different strategy should be implemented. Suppose, for example, the subject is mathematics. When it becomes obvious that the tutee is not learning, then the master tutor should recruit a new tutor, this time from among the slow learners of mathematics in the school. It may well be that a student tutor with problems similar to the tutee's, but at a different level of maturity, is better able to reach the tutee. When this approach is taken, the master tutor should select a tutor of similar race and economic background to the tutee. If this strategy fails, the next alternative is to vary the race of the tutor but maintain the other variables.

While the tutorial adjustment is being made, another junior high student should be invited into the program in order for the original tutor to have another tutee. A student tutor should not be considered a failure merely because he does not succeed with his first tutee. This is especially so since the tutees in this arrangement have severe and longstanding learning problems. Humane learning is an important part of the tutorial. Consequently, the needs of the tutor must rank equally with those of the tutee.

Other Models

Except for the high school model, it is usually impractical to bring the tutee to the tutor. For this reason and a host of others, when tutoring elementary children the tutor should go either to the tutee's classroom or to a tutorial location near his home base.

On the matter of tutoring in the elementary school, elementary teachers are about equally divided on whether they prefer high school or junior high school student tutors. Some feel that the narrower the teaching gap the better; others feel that the additional maturity of the high school student is an important asset and more than offsets the wider age gap. In any event, junior and senior high school students appear to be more successful as tutors of elementary children than do older elementary children. The older elementary student performs best as a tutor in informal learning situations such as nongraded classes. The direct tutorial approach works best when an older student serves as the tutor.

SUMMARY

Voltaire once wrote, "There is nothing so powerful as an idea whose time has come." Service learning as an important adjunct to the high school program is an idea whose time is now.

The major barrier to student involvement in service is the attitude of adults towards their participation. This is especially true in the field of medicine which, it so happens, contains the most opportunities for service. The schools must make a major effort to contact adult individuals whose attitudes are not hardened and to involve youth constructively in as many areas as possible.

Youth thrives on adventure, and getting young people out of the boredom of conventional classes and into service activities can be a very exciting happening.

The evidence is not yet in as to who profits the most from service learning, the person performing the service or the person who receives it. What is clear is that both profit, but in enormously different ways.

4

The Ungradedness
of It All

This chapter is divided into two parts. The first part describes the rationale, philosophy and system of nongradedness. The second is a description of the nongraded English program, and the purpose is to portray the application of the system to a particular discipline.

Between 1957 and 1959, when Dr. Conant was studying high schools in preparation for his exciting book, *The American High School Today,* there were no ungraded schools. So, he wrote about a program for graded schools.

The programs described in this book are appropriate to either graded or nongraded schools, but the school which is nongraded can obtain far more flexibility in its operation than can a school which operates rigidly from the graded concept.

The temper of the times no longer tolerates organizational juggling which usually amounts to nothing more than putting new wine in old bottles. The advantage of the nongraded school is that it offers a structure adaptable enough to encompass all the innovations relating to the new shape of learning.

The nongradedness of schooling adds zest to the new community support curriculum of the comprehensive high school. It makes the three to four hours a day which the student spends in the school building much more interesting.

In addition, a nongraded curriculum provides much better un-

derpinning to the community support curriculum than does the
graded school.

At the end of the nineteenth century, it was said of German
students that one-third went to the devil, one-third broke down,
and the remaining third went on to govern Europe. In America,
one-third of the students continue to drop out of high school.
The emphasis has been on keeping children in schools; it should
shift to getting them out. I am not talking here about sending
them to switchblades and the streets, but about moving them
along in school at a better rate.

In the dilemma of the grade, the dull, the average, the bright
are all retarded in one way or another. The graded structure
has generated mediocrity, and the result has been to make the
grade a sort of intellectual limbo where students are slotted for
a year at a time.

The plan of a grade for every age, as a type of organization
for learning, is its convenience as an administrative device. It
serves as a comfortable compartment in which school administrators can, and do, catalog youngsters for custodial purposes.
By comparison, nongrading is an administrative prickly pear
constantly demanding that attention be given to meeting the learning needs of students.

The innovation of the nongraded high school is out of the
hothouse. What is a nongraded school? It is a school which recognizes that students should have control over their own destiny,
consequently each student plans his own program in line with his
interest, motivation, and past achievement without regard to either
grade level or sequence.

The nongraded program is a sound, logical arrangement by
which schools can take off the academic bridle which restrains
youngsters intellectually. It is an educational design planned
around an individual's readiness for learning rather than around
rigid administrative requirements based upon age and grade.

If the public schools in America are ever to achieve the ideal of
having each youngster progress with interest and enthusiasm at
his best rate of learning, then some form of non-grading must be
instituted. This leads to the shattering implication that within
the next few years every intellectually respectable high school will

have a nongraded curricula. The grade, which has been organized around stratified layers of learning, becomes flexible, permitting open-ended progress through a curriculum which is diversified.

A NATIONAL MOVEMENT

The battle lines between graded and nongraded education were clearly drawn by Henry Dyer, Vice-President of Educational Testing Service. In an address before the tenth College Board Colloquium, Mr. Dyer reported that the practice of measuring students intellectually by the grade that they have reached is not even remotely reliable. He asserted that the grade average is only an event at best and no measure of achievement at all.

The President's Science Advisory Committee has been more concerned with education than any other federal agency except the United States Office of Education, whose role is largely one of gathering educational statistics. In the effort to upgrade the teaching of science and mathematics, the Science Advisory Committee has issued several statements concerning needed changes in the schools. One of the most significant of this group's appeals for a stepped-up educational program is the request for a diverse and varied curriculum.

Following is a plea from the Science Advisory Committee for a brand of education which will be possible only when grades have been utterly eliminated from the educational scene:

> There is a great diversity in the American educational system —but not enough. For example, despite interesting experiments in advance placement, there is still too much emphasis placed on a particular number of years of schooling—there are some students for whom this number is too many, and others for whom it is too few. There is no reason to expect every student to need twelve years to graduate from high school. Experience has shown that some able and well-adjusted students can save two or more years out of the sixteen-year program without loss. Others may well and profitably study for a longer period to attain the same goal. Moreover, within a school year there is relatively little freedom of scheduling in school or college. Most subjects are

purveyed on some kind of regular calendar which allots roughly the same amount of time to each, which appears with the same periodicity and which ignores differences in learning needs or methods, or in the importance of the subject.

Students differ widely in ability and in motivation. The number of years in school, the rate of progress, and the material covered should be determined by the capacities of the individual student, not by the capacities of the average student or by the mere chance of there being other students similarly endowed to constitute a class. It is especially important to enhance the opportunities for the most gifted student. He can do some things that the less gifted can never do. He should not face obstacles in learning to do them. Where state or local practices or requirements conflict with these goals, they should be changed.[4]

LEARNING SITUATIONS ARE FLUID

Youngsters in nongraded schools are allowed to reclassify themselves according to their interests, motivation and achievement. They schedule themselves into fluid learning situations in each subject on the basis of their individual potential and competencies. Through selective acceleration, some students begin college-level work when they become tenth graders. By the same token, some students who have reached the twelfth grade need and ask for substantial amounts of remedial work in areas in which their achievement is far below standard.

The plan for continuous learning accommodates youngsters by letting them enter temporary learning situations from which they can move at any time. These *ad hoc* learning arrangements are called "phases." A phase is material organized around a stage of development with a varying time element. One student may remain in a lower phase indefinitely; another may progress rapidly into higher phases. The prime vehicle in a program of educational diversity is mobility. The student must find the paths to deeper learning always open.

---

4 President's Science Advisory Committee, *Education for the Age of Science,* U.S. Government Printing office, 1959, p. 13.

PHASED LEARNING

The system of bonding the curriculum to the needs of the individual is called phased learning. A phase is a flexible learning situation which is related directly to the achievement of the student rather than to the grade to which he has been promoted. Expressed in another way, a phase is a stage of development with a varying time element. A student who learns in a modest fashion will remain in a phase indefinitely, even a year or more. On the other hand, a rapid learner will move through several phases within a relatively short span of time. The whole notion of phasing is dedicated to the idea of change and constant advance. The purpose is to provide a more flexible learning situation better designed to accommodate individual learning.

Phasing, then, is a method of classifying courses according to difficulty and complexity of skills and materials. It is a way of putting handles on courses in order to indicate their relative degree of sophistication. This is an important principle, as the term phasing does not apply to students. Courses are phased, not students. Actually, in practice students do not view themselves as phased since many of the courses such as Individualized Reading are multiphased and since students take courses in different phase levels over a period of time. The consequence is that it is impossible for students to become stereotyped as they enroll in courses covering a range of phases. In essence, phasing is a guidance tool.

As an aid in developing courses to assist in guidance, the following definitions are used:

Phase 1 courses are designed for students who find reading, writing, speaking and thinking quite difficult and have serious problems with basic skills.

Phase 2 courses are created for students who do not have serious difficulty with basic skills but need to improve and refine them and can do so best by learning at a somewhat slower pace.

Phase 3 courses are particularly for those who have an average command of the basic language skills and would like to advance beyond these basic skills but

do so at a moderate rather than an accelerated
pace.

Phase 4 courses are for students who learn fairly rapidly
and have good command of the basic language
skills.

Phase 5 courses offer a challenge to students who have excellent control of basic skills and who are looking
for stimulating academic learning experiences.

The phasing of courses provides the student with challenging
educational experiences because he is learning at a level com-
mensurate with his ability and sophistication. This procedure has
proven to be a more realistic learning sequence and a better
motivator than the grade level promotion.

The object of shifting from age grouping to achievement grouping is to devise an educational program suited to the individual
needs and capacities of each student. No youngster should be programed in a common design; each must be scheduled as an
individual.

This realignment of students on the basis of achievement, interest and motivation brings about a major difference in course
content between the nongraded and the conventionally graded
school. The motion of the nongraded curriculum compels the
school to resort to a much wider range of materials than is used
in the graded school. Standard textbooks aimed at a grade level
are inappropriate and have been abolished. A multiplicity of material has replaced these media. A gradeless curriculum designed
for student mobility must be saturated with a variety of materials.
But motion itself is not the cure for monotony in the schools;
liveliness of image is the key.

THE PROPOSITION

Every nongraded plan should be tested against several propo-
sitions: (1) it must make possible an accurate classification of
students of near-equal achievement; (2) it must provide for frequent reclassification so that students are permitted to move forward on an individual basis as fast as they can go; (3) it must

permit the establishment of individualized goals for each student; (4) it must have standards compatible with the varying rates at which youngsters learn.

The first step, then, in recovering from decades of intellectual sloth wrought by the grade is to reclassify youngsters for learning on the basis of their interest, motivation, and achievement rather than the grade to which they have been chronologically promoted. Students are subsequently "fanned out" in a new design.

ACHIEVEMENT TESTS

A significant component for aiding students in making decisions about their programs is their performance on nationally standardized achievement tests. This data should be available to them in complete detail, as should all information in the student's record. This is an entitlement which the schools have denied students in the past. The Intelligence Quotient, which has been the measure of the past, is of no value in the nongraded school. There are many kinds of intelligence, while the I.Q. implies that there is only one.

The results of standardized achievement tests dramatically reveal the fallacy of continuing to group students into grades. In the average high school grade, only half the youngsters have the required knowledge to be in that particular grade. For example, the dispersal of achievement among students in a tenth-grade class in English will range from grade three through grade thirteen, which is the first year of college.

THE MOBILITY OF PHASING

The concept of phased learning is founded on an awareness that each of the school's students is different. None are alike. The program of studies is designed to accommodate these variances in individuals.

The multidimensional plan of grouping students by phases is designed for the more creative development of students. All students are scheduled by subjects and depth of subjects, rather than by chronological age level, grades, and a time element. The organization is highly sensitive to individual differences as they pertain to interest, motivation, and past learning.

Students performing at lower levels of efficiency are guided into a cluster-group of basic or remedial education in the area in which they are deficient. Average achievement groupings, which understandably comprise the great majority of the school's enrollment, are designated intermediate.

Students who demonstrate academic maturity by achieving above the norm are programed into depth education. Those students who are clearly superior are scheduled into "quest" education and college-level courses. In the nongraded structure, the latter groups are urged to spend considerable time in independent study and research in their search for creative and intellectual excellence.

A major objective of phase learning is to induce the student to assume more responsibility for his education. He is encouraged to develop both direction and thrust. As an incentive to greater academic maturity, elevation from one learning phase to another may be initiated at any time by the student as well as by the teacher. This should be prefaced by an academic appraisal. The evaluation must clearly show an increase in maturity in order to avoid the yo-yo effect of returning a student to the same phase. The determination to elevate is a three-way decision involving the counselor, the student, and the teacher—with the student playing the major role. Once advanced, no student should be rephased to a lower cluster except in extreme and unusual circumstances. Down-phasing has serious implications for the individual in an organization designed for forward mobility.

The curriculum, which has a degree of flamboyance and at first seems complex, is merely unrestrained. It is designed to offer a more bountiful academic fare than is conventionally permitted when students are chronologically grouped in grades.

Another reform which is spurred by nongraded education is a change in the function of the teacher. Students who are unbridled intellectually are no longer content with a passive kind of education which is mostly just "telling." Teachers must throw out the old kit bag.

Gradeless schools are moving from memorized learning and simplified explanations to the process of inquiry for each individual. What is inquiry? In its simplest form, inquiry is curiosity linked to action. In its ultimate form, it leads to the development of imagination and creativity and eventually to new discoveries for science and the humanities.

Important to the nongraded movement are recent studies which indicate that the potentialities of the human mind, still unknown, are far greater than previously supposed. Further, these studies have exploded the hoary concept that one must have an exceptional I.Q. in order to think on the creative level. The more psychologists have found to measure, the more they have found remains to be measured.

What, then, will help us release this hidden power of the total human intellect? Unbridling the student and giving depth to the curriculum will help the student realize his full potential. The school cannot supply the whole answer to the problem of the waste of human potential, but it is duty-bound to strive mightily to assume a more realistic position in effecting changes to eliminate the waste that now occurs.

STUDENTS BECOME RESPONSIBLE

Most nongraded high schools report that when they first began to ungrade the high school, one of the earliest observations of the effects of change was a difference in the attitude of the student toward learning. Almost overnight, students started taking the initiative for their own education away from the teachers. Not only did their attitudes toward learning improve, but their behavior at school underwent an amazing transformation. The need for teachers to monitor in the halls, the cafeteria, and bus-loading areas diminished; finally this problem disappeared completely as an administrative function of the school. As scholarship began to slip out of the shadows, students started assuming greater responsibility for their conduct and teachers found themselves wisely using the leftover monitoring time to develop a better brand of education.

Student behavior and attitudes have changed so greatly at many nongraded high schools that by the middle of the third year of gradeless education the school is able to abandon truancy regulations. The problem of truancy usually diminishes to the point where it finally eliminates itself. The function of the Dean of Students shifts from one of disciplinary administration to one of counseling.

Occasional discipline problems always remain, in any kind of school, but the remaining ones originate in the classroom. The indication is strong that these are generated by the teacher rather than by student.

NO LEARNING IS EQUAL

From its beginning, American education has been a conservative institution. Experimentation has not been widespread. The attitude of educators toward change can be summed up by a quotation from the great statesman Talleyrand: ". . . and above all, not too much zeal." This lack of enthusiasm for change is at the root of many of the conventional school's problems. When a school initiates a nongraded program, enthusiasm spreads throughout both the faculty and the student body. This type of program offers a structure adaptable enough to encompass all the innovations relating to the new shape of learning.

The nongraded school is based on the principle that not all students learn all things equally well or with equal speed. Neither are all equally interested in education, nor does everyone care to pursue it to the same degree.

ADVANCED PLACEMENT

The Advanced Placement Program of the College Entrance Examination Board, if administered properly, is the best model for gradeless placement at the secondary level. Placing of students without regard to the grade is based on the proposition that students of high intellectual ability and strong motivation should not be compelled to wait until they are seniors in high school to meet the challenge of advanced courses. They should be admitted whenever their academic progress permits them to do so. What is good for the advanced student is also good for the slower student. He should be placed with the same flexibility.

Gradeless education has revealed that youngsters are capable of handling much more difficult subject matter, and at earlier ages, than has previously been supposed. Bruner expresses it well with this statement: "Any subject can be taught effectively in some intellectually honest form at any stage of development."[5]

In gradeless learning, when a youngster's achievement in a particular subject is proved by a nationally standardized scholastic achievement test to be at the college level, then the student should be encouraged to enroll in the Advanced Placement Program as soon as he enters high school. An academically talented high school student who begins college courses early in his career is able to acquire a rigorous education in an open-ended Advanced Placement Program.

The evidence is abundant that colleges are placing students without prerequisite barriers. The high schools should treat barriers even more cavalierly.

College-level courses in the secondary school have a profound impact upon the entire intellectual life of a school. When they are well taught, a high school education becomes a reasonably arduous experience for some students; and such courses inspire a more vigorous program in the entire school. Moreover, nongraded application of the Advanced Placement Program is the surest way of overcoming the difficulty of inadequate preparation of the many bright youngsters found in all high schools.

When a student is adjudged eligible to study a college-level course, in lieu of a high school course in the same subject, it is incumbent upon the school to make such a course available regardless of the student's grade level. A nongraded school offers the additional dividend to small high schools of making possible sufficient numbers of students for college-level courses. By selecting students who are intellectual peers from several grades and grouping them into the same class, a school can offer courses which it dares not offer when it must group only within the grade. This kind of flexible selection and grouping offers a solution to the major problem facing schools—the education of the superior and the talented student.

The philosophy of the nongraded school does not rest solely upon the offering of college-level courses designed so that students can receive both advanced standing and college credit. The cur-

[5] Jerome S. Bruner, *The Process of Education* (Cambridge: Harvard University Press, 1960), p. 33.

riculum which is rigid in graded schools is generally loosened so that the definition of a high school subject becomes "anything that a student can study with profit and pleasure." When this outlook is applied to a high school curriculum, and students begin to move at their own pace, things begin to happen.

EARLY ADMISSIONS

The newer version of skipping a grade is more applicable to the high school. This is the Early Admissions Plan, by which students enter college at the end of their junior year in high school, thus eliminating the senior year. Leapfrogging over an entire year of work is an unsophisticated expediting technique which recognizes an unusual intellect and attempts a kind of nongraded plan; but such a traumatic approach to learning becomes extraneous when the secondary school fulfills its responsibility by collapsing the fences around learning. With learning unconfined, the gifted range deeply and widely, without having to eradicate an entire year of work or be separated from the high school at an age when they are still immature.

The Early Admissions Plan was developed in an effort to propel talented students out of small high schools with poor curriculum offerings and directly into college at the end of their junior year. Once schools adopt the philosophy and curriculum of continuous progress through a nongraded program of studies, however, it is no longer necessary to dissever the most able students in this way. They can be well educated in the flexible setting of even a small high school which is not graded.

In a nongraded school with advanced placement work, the able student can receive instruction superior to that which he would be offered in the first year of college. Most college freshmen courses are taught by student professorial assistants or by doctoral candidates. The individuals are not comparable in ability to the best high school teachers.

While the academically able student is confronted with college work in the nongraded school, the less able student, at the other extreme, must be engaged in just as vigorous a program of basic learning. Anyone who is seriously handicapped in minimum skills may remain in a basic learning cycle during his entire high school career. If he fails to master fundamental skills, he is not pushed into deeper learning which is over his head.

THE AVERAGE STUDENT

In considering the average student, and he is the roundest figure in the school, the question of his correct stimulation looms large. Why is he average in the first place? Basically, he is average because he has never been sufficiently stimulated by his school experiences. This wanderer in the academic wilderness must have a new sense of direction. His world expands in a nongraded curriculum with flexible time schedules, group and individual work, and research.

Motivation in this direction is partially supplied by impressing each student with the reality of the freedom for development which will be his.

Individual students, and especially the average, need encouragement and direction in handling this new freedom to grow. This counseling should be extended to the second and third year in high school where necessity dictates, but the primary effort is needed in the first year. In any event, it must continue until the student demonstrates a genuine awareness of his opportunities. With the addition of effective counseling to nongrading, individualized courses, flexible scheduling and a flexible campus, it seems possible to give each student, no matter what his ability, the opportunity to grow to a dynamic realization of his potentialities as a human being. This may well become the purpose of education in the future. It should be.

THE SMALL SCHOOL

An important feature of the nongraded organization is its applicability to both small and large high schools. The advantages for each school are so positive that it is difficult to conclude which size school profits more. Without seriously attempting to resolve the point in favor of one or the other, we can say that the individual student wins in either, and this is the important point.

The small school organized around a grade for each age level is unable to offer either accelerated courses for the able, or remedial courses for the handicapped, because of the few students in each grade who can qualify for either category. When a school imaginatively combines three grades and groups its student over a three-grade span instead of one, and does this on the basis of student achievement, then the small school really comes into its own. It acquires the wherewithal to offer both a broader program of studies and a program of increased depth. The curriculum becomes meaningful.

Drawing from three grades instead of one, a school can offer remedial work to students who have learning weaknesses, and advanced work to those who are ready for acceleration. Take, as an example, the small school in Arkansas which has four hundred students spread in grades six through twelve. This school can hardly pass muster with an academic program designed for only sixty-six students per grade. When the school combines the top three grades, however, and begins to realign students, it has a base of two hundred students which it can regroup into a new shape for learning. By dividing two hundred students into new groups based upon achievement rather than age, the school has a sufficient number of able students to whom advanced work can be given. This permits a superior program of studies for all students.

The psychology of secondary learning has been wrong-headed in that it has encouraged age-level grouping, cautioning that students might develop personality problems if even slightly out of their age group. This nonsense has been a major deterrent to multiple-grade grouping in the past. Most nongraded high schools report that it makes not the slightest difference to the senior doing remedial work whether he is sitting next to a sophomore or a junior student so long as he feels that the work he is doing is worthwhile and that, at last, he is learning something useful. Talented students, while more sophisticated, are equally tolerant of age differences when student companions are intellectual peers. It is not unusual to have a sophomore making the highest mark in a class composed largely of eleventh and twelfth graders. There is a stimulation that encourages performance when equal minds start to race from the same mental starting point.

There are several schemes by which students have been accelerated in conventional education, but each of these has its draw-backs. The most widely used maneuver for quickening the learning pace has been the old practice of allowing students to skip a grade. This is a primitive form of nongrading usually initiated by a mutinous parent in full rebellion against the mediocrity of the status quo. Under the plan of skipping, the student leapfrogs over an entire year of work.

The curriculum in motion provides for the elevation of a student immediately upon evidence of improved skills and increased maturity. Prompt acceleration encourages excellence. The usual delays caused by minor details relating to completion of a marking period or an attendance period are brushed aside.

THE SCHOOL ATMOSPHERE

An objective of the phase-learning organization is to motivate the student to move as rapidly as he is able from the first to the second, to the third, and even to the fifth phase of a more meaningful and more varied curriculum than is possible in a graded school. Phased learning reinforces the teaching of students as individuals rather than as members of a captive group. It permits upward mobility, properly timed for each individual.

In essence, the purpose of nongrading is to give, in a flexible perspective, all students basic education skills, and to provide depth and quest education for those who are capable of a more profound approach. To make nongrading the challenging and vitalizing force that it should be, each course must be as stimulating and productive as possible within the limitations of time (which should be flexible), space, material, and teacher ability.

A number of interesting outlooks develop in the nongraded school as the result of a flexible program. Almost the first notion to disappear is the social concern on the part of a student or his parent that the student should be placed in an advanced group because of the prestige of being in the higher group. Once students and parents become aware that the curriculum is designed for motion and that a youngster can move at any time to the highest learning cycle in the school, this concern for status grouping vanishes. Students willingly assign themselves to low-phase placement if this appears to be in their best interest.

Actually the process of mobility is evident in every youngster's schedule. If the phased program is properly operated no student will be in a single-phase in all subjects. Every student is multiphased. That is, in one subject the student may be in a high phase and in another a medium or low phase. The program recognizes that all students have learning strengths as well as weaknesses, and it is designed to accommodate these differences. The student's learning is in no way restricted, and the result is that he quickly acquires confidence in the system.

Conventional-minded educators usually express reluctance about doing away with grades because of the ease and effectiveness with which grades can be administered. They express concern over the chaos which may result when youngsters are not kept within the framework of the graded organization. Nongraded high schools across the country have found that the nongraded system is just as easy to manage as the graded system. They have not added more personnel and the staffs do not feel overburdened.

The primary purpose of education is the development of the intellect. All other aims and objectives are subordinate. Since the expansion of the mind is best achieved when the student learns to inquire and quest for knowledge on his own, inquiry becomes a major proposition in the nongraded school. Inquiry must be deliberately undertaken and systematically sustained. Every student must be trained to think logically, critically, and independently. The schools must move from memorized learning buttressed by simplified explanations to the phenomenon of inquiry for each individual. The academic atmosphere should arouse a desire for intellectual inquiry, stimulate curiosity, and encourage creativeness.

THE DELIVERY OF LEARNING

If the function of the teacher is to deliver learning, then the role of the teacher must change. The teacher in the graded school uses educational methods that were acquired years ago. These must be dispelled. Perhaps the worst of these practices is the outmoded system of the instructor providing authoritative answers to questions. Teachers must cease the endless routine of making stereotyped inquiry into material for which they have pat answers. This is about as effective as a chanting of catechism. In too many classrooms the droning pattern is no more than an exchange between the teacher and one or two students. The process implies that learning can be transacted like dry goods across a counter.

The image of the teacher thus shifts from a fountain of wisdom to a remover of roadblocks. He removes himself to the sidelines. Here he becomes a goad as the process of education moves from the antiquity of memorized learning to the modernity of intellectual inquiry.

(Actually, of course, this idea of the role of the teacher is not new. It was envisioned in the dialogues of Socrates, who contended that the teacher's occupation was not unlike the function of the midwife. The teacher should deliver learning; he should not dispense knowledge.)

According to Bloom in his *Taxonomy of Educational Objectives*, simple recall, spurred by rudimentary questions, is the lowest order of intellectual activity. The more rigorous intellectual activities going up the scale are comprehension, application, analysis, synthesis, and evaluation.

Although the use of questions by teachers has some learning value, teachers must spend more time in preparing questions. They must pose enigmas which require more than just recall. The stranglehold which simple recall has held on the classroom for centuries must be broken.

This means that the classroom activity which has been structured around a feedback of passive citation of facts must move toward a problem-solving atmosphere. I realize that when we speak of discarding the teaching of facts, we are talking about abolishing something which is on a par with motherhood, football, and the United States Marines, and that this methodology is counted by many people as among the first ten American blessings. But with knowledge being doubled in some areas every decade, these schools must abandon the fruitless task of trying to cover facts and shift the emphasis to the realistic development of curiosity, intellectual inquiry, and intuitive thinking. We must go beyond the teaching of facts to what Whitehead calls "the imaginative consideration of facts."

Students in nongraded high schools must be taught to analyze important and erudite monographs weighted with conflicting opinions. They must be rigorously exposed to interpretive study. They must learn that there are always more questions than there are answers, and that the quest for answers is exciting, vital, and worthy of a life's dedication. They must assume much greater direction and control over their own learning activities.

Teaching has been thought of as handing out knowledge and transmitting the culture of young learners. If hemophilia had been transmitted by anything so unreliable, there would surely be no such disease. The favorite performance, the lecture method, is the teacher's right arm—and the poorest of all techniques for teaching. Its role in the school must move from a major to a minor one.

THE NONGRADED ENGLISH PROGRAM

The first nongraded English program was established at Melbourne High School in Melbourne, Florida, as a part of that school's development as the first nongraded high school. Since that time there have been hundreds of adaptations of this program, usually with very slight modifications. Perhaps the most extensive hitchhike on the Melbourne development is the evolvement of a nongraded English program at Trenton High School in Trenton, Michigan.

The Trenton program, widely known as project APEX, Appropriate Placement for Excellence in English, was initially heavily funded by the U.S. Office of Education. As a result, the school has been able financially to distribute thousands of free books describing the program. For this reason the Apex curriculum in English is probably better known than the English program of any other nongraded high school. Since the Apex curriculum is at best a hybrid development adapted from the Appropriate Placement program of Melbourne High School, I feel that more insight into the application of nongradedness can be obtained from an examination of the original development.

The following description was written by Mrs. Elizabeth Williams, Phi Beta Kappa graduate of Wake Forest College and a teacher of English at Melbourne High School:

The Unequal Treatment of Unequals:
The English Program at Melbourne High School

by Elizabeth Williams

I. Introduction: The Phase System

II. The Program for the Slow Learner

  A. Phase I
   1. Student characteristics
   2. Objectives
   3. Physical facilities and materials
   4. Teaching methods
   5. Evaluation and credit

  B. Phase II
   1. Student characteristics
   2. Objectives
   3. Materials
   4. Teaching methods
   5. Evaluation and credit

III. The Program for the Average Student—Phase III

  A. Basic differences between Phase II and Phase III
  B. Student characteristics
  C. Objectives
  D. The Literature Cycle
  E. Materials
  F. Teaching methods
  G. Evaluation and credit
  H. Elective courses

IV. The Program for the Advanced Student

  A. Phase IV.
   1. Basic differences between average and advanced programs
   2. Student characteristics
   3. Objectives
   4. Teaching methods
   5. Materials

        6. Sample units of study
        7. Evaluation and credit

    B. Phase V
        1. Student characteristics
        2. Objectives
        3. Teaching methods
        4. Materials
        5. Evaluation and credit
        6. Advanced Placement English

V. The Independent Study Program

VI. Conclusions

THE PHASE SYSTEMS

Dr. B. Frank Brown, Melbourne High School's former principal and innovator of its non-graded system, embodies the philosophy of the school in his belief that "there is nothing so unequal as the equal treatment of unequals." In its efforts to treat unequals unequally, Melbourne High operates on the phase system, a system whereby students are placed in classes on the basis of past achievement in a particular subject rather than on chronological age.

The belief that a phased curriculum offers each student learning that is within his own individual reach forms the basis for the structure of the entire academic program at Melbourne High. The English Department at the school, involving approximately 2,200 students and eighteen teachers, is the largest unit within this structure. In its curriculum, there are no tenth, eleventh, and twelfth grade English courses, for there are no tenth, eleventh, and twelfth grades. There are, instead, five "phases" or learning situations from which a student can move at any time. Each phase represents a different level of achievement and each one differs in the approach to the subject matter itself and in the depth at which mastery is anticipated.

The Phase I English program is designed to provide the student with remedial work in basic skills. Phase II English is designed for developing existing, but limited skills. Phase III classes are for students of moderate ability. Phase IV English involves in-depth study for above-average students; and Phase V English, a highly advanced course, is for students capable of doing college level work in high school. In addition to these five levels, there is Phase Q—for "Quest"—which is an independent study program.

An individual student's phase in English is determined primarily by achievement scores in reading, grammar, and spelling on standardized tests such as Stanford. Previous performance in class and style of learning are also taken into consideration when these factors are known.

When a student enters the school, he is given a statement of his recommended phase level in English, but he is not obligated to take the suggested level course. If he elects to up-phase, then he is allowed to determine if he can meet the challenge. If he down-phases then he must live with the consequences of possible boredom. But the final choice of phase level lies with the student. The only restriction is that a student who achieves at an average level or better in English is not allowed to take a Phase I or Phase II English course.

Since three units of English are required for graduation from Melbourne High, most students take an English course each of their three years at the school. Many students stay in the same phase level all three years; others move back and forth as they seek to find the level at which they can best learn or as their achievement level rises or falls.

When students' test scores in reading and related subjects fall below the 20th percentile, the individualized program of study which the Phase I Reading Lab offers is usually recommended for them. Low-achieving students, however, are not placed in Phase I simply on the basis of test scores. Diverse as these students are in ability, background, and nature, they have some traits in common which aid in further identifying them as applicants for this program. They are usually reading at about the third to fifth grade level and are extremely weak in speaking, listening, and writing skills. Because of previous failure, they may have a negative feeling toward school in general and may exhibit no aspirations for success in the academic program. Moreover, the Phase I students are frequently less stable emotionally than the more motivated learners and often lack a favorable self-image. Such students have a very short attention span and show little perseverance. Because of these and similar problems, low-achievers need immediate and continuous reinforcement from the teacher and constant reassurance of their relationship with the teacher and with the subject matter.

Given a student with some or all of the foregoing characteristics, the Phase I English Program seeks to help him to develop to his highest potential, always considering his talents and limitations. Consequently, the program sets for itself the following objectives:

1. To keep potential dropouts in school and to provide a rescue operation in the form of a program tailored as much as possible to their needs.
2. To challenge the potential dropout by utilizing his immediate interests and his future hopes for life after school.
3. To help the students discover success.
4. To increase their ability to read.
5. To help the students learn how to get a job.
6. To help the students discover that learning can be a genuinely interesting and enjoyable activity.
7. To help the students gain respect for one another. ·
8. To help the students discover practical communication skills.
9. To help the students discover a self-image that is favorable to them.
10. To help the students acquire wider vision about the use of leisure time.

Because physical facilities and materials play a major role in achieving these objectives, the Phase I English Program removes the student from the traditional classroom atmosphere, where he is restricted to one chair, and places him in more sophisticated physical surroundings. Melbourne High's large reading laboratory offers the student easy chairs, informal classroom arrangements, excellent lighting, air-conditioning, carpeted floors, and other small luxuries conducive to study.

The reading lab facility includes a large reading room and three instructional rooms. The large reading room has study carrels, several easy chairs, and tables with chairs for small group work. Located here also is the free reading library which consists of five hundred paperback and hardback books plus an adequate supply of magazines. The instructional rooms have several desks for individual study and also house such audio-visual equipment as overhead projectors, record players, tape recorders, and reading machines.

Because the Phase I program is highly individualized, a diversity of textbooks and other materials is used. The basic texts are the Follett Publishing Company collections: the *Turner-Livingston Communication Series, Accent Personality Series,* and *World of Work Series.* These collections are alternated in a three-year cycle to prevent repetition of reading materials. In addition to these and the paperbacks and *Readers Digest,* various spelling, grammar, and vocabulary workbooks are used as needed by individual students.

The Phase I program is supervised by one teacher who works with approximately fifteen students per period. Of primary importance to the teacher-student relationship is the maintenance of an informal, relaxed classroom atmosphere, for the right environment is imperative to low-phase learning. The students must be encouraged to contribute, discuss, and ask questions in class.

Special effort is made by the teacher to confer frequently with each student in order to help him move along in his own special way. Conference results are kept in special student files which also contain a record of the student's progress in reading and composition. These records are the primary sources used in evaluating and grading the student.

Because low achievers frequently respond to negative marks of evaluation with apathy and lessened productivity, a traditional grading system is not used. In the lab, the student is either progressing or he is maintaining the status quo in his achievement. If he is progressing, the grade of "satisfactory" is given. Many devices which are more challenging to the student than is the grade, however, are available to the teacher daily to show evaluative approval or disapproval of a student's efforts.

Phase I students receive one credit in English for spending one hour a day for a year in the lab. The lab program is the only one in English open to the Phase I level student. Because his needs are so basic and so demanding, no elective courses are offered on the Phase I level.

The Phase II Communication Skills program is recommended for students who score between the 21st and 40th percentile in reading and related subjects on standardized tests. The Phase II student may be further identified as one who reads between the sixth and tenth grade level and who needs more emphasis on the basic skills. Moreover, students at this achievement level will generally demonstrate some or all of the following characteristics:

1. They have a history of failing academic grades and poor attendance in school.
2. They are either brash and overcompensating or reticent and retiring in class.
3. They usually display aptness in peer group sociability.
4. They respond well to manipulative tasks.
5. They have a restricted, but expanding, vocabulary.
6. They work better with the concrete and experience difficulty with the abstract.
7. They have negative feelings toward school.
8. They are not self-confident with the subject matter.
9. They need continuing reinforcement in their work and in their teacher-student relationships.
10. They often lack faith in themselves and in those other than their own peer group.

To develop the potential of a student with some or all of these characteristics, the Phase II program sets as general objectives: the expansion of the limits of the student's reading interest areas and the depth of his perception within these areas; increasing the student's ability to understand and evaluate the information he receives through the mass media; the development within the student of an awareness of the dangers involved in not being able to understand the information which conditions his thinking and behavior; and helping the student to express his thoughts clearly in speaking and writing.

More specifically, the Phase II program concentrates on individual improvement in basic communication skills. It seeks to improve reading speed and accuracy as well as comprehension, to enlarge the reading vocabulary, to teach the student to read for main ideas and for particular facts, to develop his ability to write with variety in sentence structure, to improve his spelling and punctuation, and to help develop creativity and originality. In the areas of speaking and listening skills, the course tries to help the student understand the need for correct speech, to help him learn to enjoy speaking situations, to help him learn to speak with confidence, and to help him develop critical listening skills. Improvement of library skills is also stressed in the Phase II program.

As in the Phase I program, the Phase II Communication Skills program is housed in the Reading Laboratory. Again, classes in this phase are quite small. The Phase II staff consists of a two-teacher team with two paramedia specialists and two student assistants. This group works with about forty-five students at a time.

Some Phase II students spend two hours a day in the lab. During the first hour, the staff works with them on phonetics skills, vocabulary, spelling and grammar. During the second hour, students concentrate on improving reading skills through directed reading of assigned literature or, occasionally, through free reading. Under teacher guidance, students work in small groups, often reading the literature aloud and then discussing it. Stress is also placed on improving their ability to respond to literature in writing. These students receive one credit in English for spending two hours in the lab per semester.

Other Phase II students spend only one hour a day in the lab. They undertake a similar program and receive one-half credit in English per semester.

All of the lab's books, machines, and other materials are available to the Phase II student. The basic texts for this phase are Silver Burdett's *Success in Reading, Books 1–4, Merrill Mainstream Literature Series,* and other literature books geared to this level student. *Scope* is also used.

Since Phase II students need a structured situation, teachers are very careful to let them know what is expected of them. Individual conferences are held as often as possible. Continual diagnosis and evaluation of the student's problems in the area of communication skills are made in order to improve specific individual reading difficulties and skill deficiencies. Concise records of the student's progress are kept and are used for evaluation.

The ultimate goal of the Phase II program is to so improve the student's reading, writing, and speaking skills that he can move out of the lab situation and into a Phase III classroom. If, within a semester's time, he has so progressed, he receives a grade of "satisfactory" and up-phases. If he is not progressing, he is given a grade of "unsatisfactory" and continues in the lab program.

For the Phase II student, the Communication Skills course is the required course, the only one which will satisfy the graduation requirement. There are no elective courses on this level.

Phase III English has several significant distinctions from Phase II. It has far more subject-matter structure; therefore, its orientation is far more subject-matter centered. More attention is paid to form and style in literature as well as in composition. A course of this nature comes close to resembling a reasonably "typical" English class, with its concomitant activities and expectations. Consequently, the Phase III program is designed to accommodate students who fall into a middle or "average" category.

The student for whom this phase is recommended usually ranks between the 41st and 60th percentile on the Stanford Achievement Test. He is reading at about the ninth- to eleventh-grade level. There are, moreover, certain identifying characteristics which may be noted in the Phase III students which help point up their needs. These students may be outspoken, often responding strongly, immediately, and sometimes negatively to assignments, tests, and classroom activities. They are likely to be strongly influenced by their peer group and will exhibit a concern for the immediate and the pragmatic. A common question in relation to reading and other assignments in a Phase III class is, "What's this got to do with me?" But their attention span and their skill development may be erratic. These students learn well in a highly verbal situation, but find difficulty in individual pursuits. They are capable of concrete visualization, but have problems with abstractions, particularly in moving inductively from concrete facts to abstract hypotheses. They need, therefore, redundant teacher direction and explanation.

Since the Phase III student is at least moderately involved in his learning process, much more can be expected in terms of intellectual skills with this student than with the Phase II student, as is exhibited in the objectives of the course. In general the Phase III program seeks to get the student involved in the study of English by helping him to appreciate the relevance of it to the world in which he lives. It further seeks to promote student initiative, originality, and imagination and to assist the student to become a self-directed learner. It tries to help the student to reason logically, defend his ideas from the material studied, and to impart these ideas to others orally or in writing.

More specifically, the Phase III course is concerned with developing the following skills:

1. Reading: understanding of the literary genre and the terminology connected with each genre; improvement in comprehension and interpretation of works read; development of ability to analyze in some detail works read.

2. Writing: improvement of sentence and paragraph structure; development of good word usage and precision in word choice; introduction to the forms of discourse and to the elements of style; development of research techniques; improvement of spelling and expansion of vocabulary.

3. Speaking and listening: improvement in giving various types of speeches; development of active participation in small group discussions; introduction to techniques of debate and of parliamentary procedure.

The Phase III program also seeks to help the student to learn to use the library with skill and ease.

Since many of the students for whom the Phase III objectives are geared take Phase III English for three years, the program operates on a three-year cycle to avoid repetition in any aspect of the curriculum. Each year's program is structured around one area of literary study: World Literature, American Literature, or British Literature. Students entering the school in a given school year will take World Literature. In the following school session, British Literature will be taught, and the session after that will feature American Literature. Likewise, the language and composition programs of study are varied each year so that no major unit of study is repeated in a three-year period.

To best implement this varied program, teachers work in teams of three, with one of the three serving as team head. In the current Phase III system, there are three teams: a low Phase III team, a regular Phase III team, and a high Phase

III team. Each team has a common planning period so that teachers can work out lesson plans and discuss ideas together. Unlike the Phase I and Phase II programs, members of a team do not share a common room or rooms. Each teacher has her own classroom, some equipped with chair-desks and some with tables and chairs grouped to accommodate six to eight students around a table. Whenever possible, a team is given adjacent rooms so that materials and equipment can easily be shared. Each team has a record player, an overhead projector, a tape recorder and other audio-visual equipment when needed.

All Phase III classes use identical textbooks; each student has his own literature text, his own language text and his own composition text for the year's work. For the World Literature study, the McGraw-Hill *Literature of the World* is used together with Ginn's *Writing: Unit Lessons in Composition, Book 1, C,* and American Book Company's *Modern Grammar and Composition Book Two.* For the American Literaure study, the text is Harcourt, Brace and World's *Adventures in American Literature* used together with *Book 2, C* of the Ginn composition series and the same language text, but different sections emphasized. The program uses Harcourt, Brace and World's *Adventures in English Literature* for the British Literature study together with *Book 3, C* of the Ginn series and different sections of the language text. In addition to the texts, paperback copies of novels and plays are used in the literature study.

Varied teaching techniques are used in the Phase III classroom. Small group discussion is used often as this level student is more likely to express his ideas to his peers than to his teacher. However, the large class discussion is sometimes employed. Individual study and research are part of the program and the classes make much use of the library and its facilities.

Although the Phase III program is structured around the literature, teachers recognize the necessity for emphasis on improvement of writing techniques and on language study. Approximately two weeks of each six-week grading period are given to work in these areas. As much as possible, the writing and language programs are integrated with the current literature study.

Approaches to the study of literature are varied for each

year's program. World Literature is structured around different countries and/or areas. For the first semester, the three units of study are: French Literature and library research skills; Italian, Spanish and Portuguese literature and diagnosing of composition weaknesses; Scandinavian and German literature and grammar skills. The second semester program continues emphasis on composition skills with Russian, Hebrew, Roman, Greek, and Asian literature studied.

The British literature study is organized by genre. In the first semester, the students are concerned with the essay, the drama, and the short story. The second semester study begins with the novel and concludes in the spring with poetry. Various units of language and composition study from the texts are integrated with the literature program.

The unit of organization for the American Literature study is the theme. Beginning in the fall and moving into the spring, works relating to the following themes are analyzed: The American Puritan Attitude, The American Desire for Success, American Romanticism, The American Darker Spirit, The American Social Conscience, and The American Quest for Identity. Works covered will vary from team to team in keeping with the achievement level of the students, but all teams are concerned with the same theme at the same time.

Because the Phase III program is a more structured and "typical" one than the Phase I and Phase II programs, a more traditional form of grading is employed here. Phase III students receive an "A" for excellent work, a "B" for good work, a "C" for average work, and a "D" for poor work. If a student is not progressing according to his potential at all, he receives an "F" and no credit for the course. When failure occurs, reasons for it are analyzed by teachers, who may sometimes recommend that a student down-phase.

The Phase III student must take the World, British, and American Literature courses to receive his three credits in English for graduation. If, however, he wishes to take additional English courses on the Phase III level, the following electives are available to him: Drama, Speed Reading, Journalism, and Composition. Also, to accommodate students who may come from other schools where they have already had the particular literature study being offered in any year, a Phase III class in one of the other literary areas is available.

The English program for the advanced student—Phases IV and V—differs from its Phase III counterpart in breadth as well as depth. It differs significantly in the expectations of student response as well as the sophistication that is to accompany the response. Where a Phase III class might well deal with the "whatness" of things, Phases IV and V will deal with the "whyness" of things. Whereas a Phase III class will examine what a piece of literature means, Phases IV and V will examine why the author did what he did in order to achieve a particular meaning. A much greater emphasis is placed on the higher cognitive processes, such as analysis, synthesis, and evaluation. It is fully expected that generalizations will be made from the literary situation to a concrete life situation, to another literary situation, or to an abstraction that might have a reasonable degree of universal application. Analyzation of works in depth is expected and once the analysis has been done, synthesis, followed by a well-supported, documented evaluation, should be achieved.

Writing in these programs is accompanied by a greater emphasis on a sense of style, on the use of appropriate diction, as well as the use of descriptive words and phrases to augment and highlight the writing itself. The language study is highly student-writing centered. The application of the structural approach to the writing problems of the classroom is effected by having the student analyze his own writing and the writing of others for errors that hinder the effectiveness of communication.

The student should function well in the Phase IV environment if he is one who scores between the 61st and 80th percentiles on the Stanford or similar achievement tests and who reads at tenth grade level or above. To avoid error in placement, however, other identifying characteristics are considered. The Phase IV student is usually highly concerned with academic competition, is very grade-conscious, and may be under parental pressure to succeed. Having already some well-developed skills in subject matter, he is ready for depth of penetration into literature and for experimentation with various kinds of writing. His independence is such that he requires only occasional teacher direction.

To assist this type of student in achieving his highest potential in English, the Phase IV program has the following objectives for the student:

1. Literature: to gain in-depth understanding of the novel, short story, essay, drama, and poetry; to analyze literature in relation to cultural and literary heritage; to determine the intent and the tone of a writer's work; to distinguish between fact and a statement of opinion, between unsupported opinion and judgment based on evidence; to analyze the meanings of words in their context to facilitate complete understanding; to determine the effect of integration of plot, character, style, and setting on the theme of a literary work; to identify the characteristics of a literary movement; to analyze the relationship between an author's work, his life, and the times in which the work was written.

2. Writing, Speaking and Listening: to develop ability to express ideas orally; to continue vocabulary development; to learn to use appropriate language, organization, and tone for different audiences and situations; to develop competence in expository, descriptive, narrative, and argumentative writing; to concentrate on refining a work which begins as a first draft; to summarize orally and in writing the main ideas of a difficult passage of prose; to listen in order to follow the sequence of ideas, to determine the main idea, and to respond meaningfully to an oral presentation.

To accomplish such objectives as these, the Phase IV program employs the three-year literary cycle. Both Phases IV and V are concerned with the same area of literature study each year as is the Phase III program and the same method of approach (World: countries; British: genre, American: theme) is employed in these phases. Therefore, all Phase III, Phase IV and Phase V English students are involved in the same American Literature theme, the same British Literature genre, or the same World Literature country at the same time. Such organization enables students to move from one phase to another within the school year without repeating an area of study.

The Phase IV program involves about four hundred and fifty students and a team of four teachers. The teachers have individual classrooms which are adjacent to each other. They have a common planning period in which they discuss lesson plans, share ideas, and seek to solve common problems. They teach five classes a day of approximately twenty-five to thirty students each.

Teaching methods are similar to those discussed in the Phase III program except that there is much less teacher direction in a Phase IV classroom. Much use is made of the small group discussion, the panel discussion, and individual study and research followed by a written or oral report. More so than the Phase III student, the Phase IV student can profit from short lectures, and this technique is occasionally employed. Since Phase IV students are quite apt verbally, they generally participate well in large class discussions, whether teacher-led or student-led. Teachers make use of record players, tape recorders, overhead projectors, and other audio-visual aids to a great extent, especially in the teaching of language and composition.

The writing and language texts for the Phase IV program are in the same series as those used in the Phase III course, but they are on a more advanced level than are the lower phase ones. The *B* series of the Ginn book, *Writing: Unit Lessons in Composition,* is the standard writing text, with books one, two, and three in the series alternated in a three-year cycle. The American Book Company's *Modern Grammar and Composition, Book Three* is the language text, a more advanced language study than that of *Book Two* which is used in Phase III.

For the World Literature study, the Phase IV text is *Insight: The Experience of Literature,* published by Noble and Noble. For British Literature, Scott, Foresman's *England in Literature* is used, and for American Literature, the same company's *The United States in Literature* is the anthology.

In each of the three literary studies, the text serves primarily as a means of instilling a sense of the chronological development of the literature in the students and as a source for essays, short stories, and poems. Large numbers of paperback copies of plays and novels and collections of shorter works, which the students purchase themselves, are used to supplement the texts.

Implementation of these materials in the Phase IV program might best be indicated by describing a sample unit of study for one six-week period: the American Puritan Attitude theme in the American Literature course. Students begin with some introductory writing work, including a study of library and research techniques, which culminates in a short research paper on some aspect of Puritanism. They read Arthur Miller's *The Crucible* in paperback, write a class paper on it, and also take a test on the play. This is followed by a study of Hawthorne's *The Scarlet Letter,* also read in paperback and discussed in small groups in class. A paper is written on this novel and then Hawthorne's short story, *Young Goodman Brown,* is analyzed. Short selections by the early Puritan writers from the text are discussed in class and the unit concludes with a week of language study from the American Book Company text.

Recently a unit of study on Mass Media has been incorporated into the Phase IV program. During the 1968–69 study of American Literature, Phase IV students explored the American Social Conscience through musical drama and films. After studying techniques involved in producing musicals and films, after reading musical dramas and listening to the music, and after viewing a number of films, the students were asked to write, direct, act or film their own original work. Working in groups, they produced one full-scale musical, complete with original costumes, sets, words and music, and about twenty films, concerned with topics ranging from "The Sunday Christian" to the evils of over-eating. The students have indicated that they like such different and creatively challenging units of study and more of this type of program will probably be incorporated into the English courses in the future.

Evaluation of the Phase IV student is similar to that of the Phase III student. He, too, is graded "A," "B," "C," "D" and "F," depending on his progress according to his potential. Like the Phase III student, he must take the three required literature courses to receive his English credits for graduation. However, if he wishes to take additional English courses, Phase IV courses in Drama and Composition are open to him. There is also available each year a Phase IV class in one of the areas of literature other than that being emphasized that year.

Phase V English differs from Phase IV only to the extent that more of all the qualities expected in the Phase IV student are anticipated in the Phase V student. The response is expected to be sharper, more defined, and more polished. If Phase IV can be called "advanced," then Phase V can be called "more advanced" or a college-level course in high school.

More specifically, the Phase V program is designed to accommodate students who score between the 81st and 99th percentiles on standard achievement tests and who are reading at twelfth-grade level or above. Moreover, Phase V students demonstrate a high degree of self-motivation and intellectual curiosity to its highest potential. To do this, it sets the following general objectives for the student: achieving mastery of the tools and techniques of research; becoming familiar with critical techniques applicable to various literary genre and becoming discriminating in analysis of literature; recognizing the various propaganda techniques utilized by the different media to influence public decisions; analyzing literary works with great depth of penetration of meaning; improving ability to write and speak with conviction and intellectual honesty; strengthening overall language development by extensive vocabulary study and gaining knowledge of stylistic techniques.

In order to accomplish these objectives in a similar way for all Phase V students, the Phase V program has only one teacher. She teaches five classes of approximately twenty-five students per class. Her classes meet in a room equipped with tables and chairs arranged for small group discussions of about six to eight students. She employs an informal, seminar technique for class discussions and seeks to serve more as catalyst than autocrat. Many of the assignments she gives are of an individual nature, requiring the students to assume a great degree of personal responsibility. She makes use of audio-visual aids (especially records and films) to some extent. She schedules teacher-student conferences at regular intervals to discuss the student's progress (or lack of it) and to go over his writing assignments in detail with him.

As do Phases III and IV, the Phase V program makes use of a writing, language and literature text for each student. The writing text is Ginn's *Unit Lessons in Composition, A* level, with books one, two and three alternating in a three-year cycle. The language text is the most advanced of the American Book Company's series, *Resources for Modern Grammar and Composition, Book 4.* The text for World Literature is Harcourt, Brace and World's *Adventures in World Literature.* For British literature, the same company's *Major British Writers: Shorter Edition* is employed. The literature texts are supplemented with paperback copies of plays, novels, and collections of shorter works.

The Phase V student is evaluated and graded in a manner similar to that used in Phases III and IV. His evaluation is based on the amount of progress he has made in relation to his potential and he receives a letter grade to indicate excellent, good, average, poor, or failing work.

Although there are no electives offered on the Phase V level, Phase V students sometimes take the Journalism or Drama or Composition courses offered on the Phase III and IV levels. However, unlike the other phases, Phase V offers an alternate course to the World, British, and American Literature cycle which also satisfies the English graduation requirement. This course, Advanced Placement English, differs from the regular Phase V program only in the content of the course. Its subject matter is not restricted to any one of the three areas of literary study but rather cross-cuts them, concentrating heavily on British and American works, but including other major works in translation. Unlike the other courses, the Advanced Placement course operates on a two-year cycle, since sophomores seldom enroll for it. There is only one class of about twenty-five students, most of whom are interested in taking the Advanced Placement Examinations offered nationally in May of each year.

The Advanced Placement course has no prescribed textbook. Instead, it uses paperbacks for the study of both literature and writing. Although the content of the course and the books selected will vary with whoever is teaching it, the teacher is careful to select works that are not used in any of the other English programs. A typical Advanced Placement program for a year's study might resemble the following:

First Semester:

I.   The Heroic Mode

The Greek Myths
The Odyssey—Homer
Selections from *Don Quixote*—Cervantes
Selections from *Paradise Lost*—Milton
Prometheus Bound—Aeschylus

II. The Tragic Mode

Oedipus Rex—Sophocles
King Lear—Shakespeare
Ghosts—Ibsen
Desire Under the Elms—O'Neill
Death of a Salesman—Miller
The Mayor of Casterbridge—Hardy
Wuthering Heights—Bronte
The Book of Job
Essays on Tragedy

Second Semester:

I.   The Comic Mode

Troilus and Criseyde—Chaucer
Emma—Austen
The Natural—Malamud
The Tempest—Shakespeare
Volpone—Jonson
School for Scandal—Sheridan
The Devil's Disciple—Shaw
Essays on Comedy

II. The Lyric Mode

Paperback anthologies of both classical
    and modern poetry
Lyrical dramas and short stories

As do all the English programs, the Advanced Placement program seeks to develop the student's ability to write clearly and logically and to develop his sensitivity to nuances in the use of language. Prentice-Hall's *Thinking Straight* and *Writing Themes About Literature* are often used in the course to help accomplish these purposes.

Although Advanced Placement and all the other English programs at Melbourne High seem to be highly structured, both teachers and students are given much freedom to develop their individual interests. Although the textbooks are prescribed by the county, the paperbacks are not, and individual teachers select favorite plays and novels to discuss with their students. Although teams work closely together, a teacher is free in her own classroom to use whatever teaching aids and whatever approaches to the material she wishes to use. Although the student is required to take the three literature courses, he also is free to choose the level on which he wishes to pursue these studies and to select the teachers with whom he wishes to work. He also has a selection of elective courses to delve into if he wishes to pursue certain areas of study in more detail.

The zenith of freedom for the student, however, lies in the independent study program, where he can create his own course. Working with a teacher one hour a day in the library, he tailors his study completely to his own desires and motivation. Here, he may concentrate on creative writing or work on improving his vocabulary. He may do a depth study of Greek Tragedy, modern American poetry, or the Theater of the Absurd. *Whatever* his interests in the field of English, he may pursue them under teacher guidance in the independent study program. His teacher evaluates his work, grades his papers, and gives him a letter grade for his course. The independent study program gives only elective credit; it cannot be substituted for the required courses.

Students in any phase in English may do independent study. One English teacher is given one period a day to work with independent study students in the library. These students decide on the topic for study, prepare a list of resource materials available in the library, structure their course of study, and turn in at regular intervals work to be evaluated by the teacher. About fifteen to twenty students are involved in independent study in English at one time.

Thus, the independent study program is the culmination of the phase system's ultimate goal: the individualization of learning. What the system seems to be accomplishing at present for the student of English is allowing him to perform at his own level, to move at his own pace, and to achieve a sense of satisfaction in accomplishment. For the teachers of English, it seems to be transforming them from authorities on World, British, or American Literature into authorities on a particular type of student with particular characteristics and particular learning problems who requires particular materials and particular teaching methods in order to learn. The system is treating unequals unequally.

5

Independent Study
in the Comprehensive High School

The "college without walls" which has proven so successful in Great Britain is rapidly being introduced into the United States. Under this concept an individual can pursue any curriculum which he chooses, mostly in his own home, on his own time and at his own pace. Rarely is he required to attend specific classes at definite locations. The nub of the matter is that the individual learns on his own, almost completely outside of the normal institutional framework.

In the vanguard of this program is the state of Massachusetts, which plans a full scale inauguration in 1972. If the program proves as successful as the governor anticipates, then taxpayers will be spared the enormous expense of building an ever increasing number of buildings and campuses in years to come. In the words of Governor Sargent, "The chance to get a higher education in Massachusetts—indeed in America—has, for too long, been tied to a brick-and-mortar mentality and to a student's ability to pay for learning."

The "college without walls" is also spreading to other areas, and New York State is following closely behind Massachusetts. New York State's newest university, the Empire State College, is based on the assumption that learning occurs in highly diverse situations. The resources at Empire State College will not be limited to a classroom or campus, according to its planners.

Learning will take place beyond the walls of a campus, amid the realities of everyday life. A temporarily vacated college dormitory will do; an old house in the country is ideal; an off-season motel or hotel, if sufficiently inexpensive, can serve. The significant thing for such short-term intensive sessions is not what the facilities have to offer, but what the persons bring to the facilities and create for themselves while they are there.

The implementaton of the "college without walls" program has enormous implications for radical reform of the high school curricula. The short range inference is for a new and extensive emphasis on curricula which helps students to learn how to learn. Once an individual has achieved this goal, he can continue college and university work while remaining in his own community. The long range connotation is that the "college without walls" will bring on an era of "high schools without walls." Before this can become a fait accompli, however, the junior high and elementary schools will have to accomplish a great deal more in the way of helping students to learn how to learn. Only then can we successfully have "high schools without walls."

With this objective in mind, every high school faculty should adopt as a major goal the purpose of developing students who not only have learned how to learn but who are willing to accept the major responsibility for their own learning. When students assume direction of their learning time, they learn not simply a great deal more subject matter but they also learn other things of great value. Furthermore, their opportunities for learning from a variety of sources are greatly enhanced.

Highly individualized independent learning opportunities should be open to all students who can handle themselves in learning situations which do not require pressure. Furthermore, independent study should begin as early as the student can cope with it. Avant-garde schools have already established a trend of making independent learning more and more available to increasing numbers of students.

The more able students should be privileged to elect the most independent programs, and all students should have varying degrees of independence. The obvious value of having students learn how to learn on their own, instead of being constantly directed by authority, is so apparent that every school should find it worth while to tackle this difficult problem. It is high time for teachers to become accustomed to seeing students "out of their regular places." When this happens, students and teachers will become "associates" in education, rather than adversaries.

The gist of the matter is that the conventional wisdom of the classroom is being assailed—learning is something that people do for themselves. Nor can schools make learning happen without the cooperation of the learner—learning can no longer be built around the teacher and the book.

FORMULA FOR INNOVATION

When a school expands into broad comprehensiveness, offering independent study and service and work-study programs for all students, it encounters the same problems as any school anywhere in adopting an innovation. It must follow a set of procedures which will lead to reform. In order to assist schools to plan for independent study or any other major reform, the following guidelines are suggested:

1. Current program—The school assesses its program of studies analyzing what it has accomplished in the past.
2. Capability—The assessment of its present program should be focused against the faculty potential for either adopting or developing new programs.
3. Weaknesses—Particular attention should be given to eliminating weaknesses before an innovation is attempted. For example, if the school has poor community support, this should be improved, either before, or in conjunction with, the launching of the new program.
4. Strengths—The more positive and creative aspects of the school's faculty and existing curriculum and organization should be marshalled to support the planned innovation.
5. The Consumer—Students should be involved in the planning from the very beginning. Their support can be the decisive factor in success.

IMPLEMENTATION PLAN

1. Feasibility—The appropriateness of the new program to the student body and the ability of the staff to manage it must receive major consideration.
2. Objectives—Clear and measurable objectives should be established. This does not refer to the nebulous behavioral type objectives, but to down-to-earth concrete goals.
3. Evaluation—Continuous evaluation with well-established checkpoints for more careful analysis should be a vital part of the new program.
4. Alternatives—Alternate strategies should be established and ready to implement if the initial thrust does not attain the desired results.

THE FEDERAL ROLE

The impact of federal participation in school programs has been all to the good with the exception of its participation in vocational education. This latter has been so fraught with rules and regulations that it has been largely ineffective. The government's contribution to the development of independent study has been quite positive.

The history of government involvement in education is short. There was no involvement prior to the launching of the Russian Sputnik in October of 1957. Even then the first federal aid was passed under the guise of defense and was even called the National Defense Education Act.

The passage of Title III a decade later had a highly beneficial effect as long as the U.S. Office of Education was making grants for innovative programs directly to school districts, bypassing the bureaucratic state departments of education. During this era, nongraded and independent study programs received enormous emphasis and the schools took a mighty leap forward. Unfortunately, Congress bowed to pressure from the states after several years and now grants the money through the state departments of education. For all of the impact of federal funds since the funding started going through the states, they may as well keep it. Much of the money is now spent at the state level and state departments of education are notoriously uncreative. The gist of the matter is that since federal funding has been channeled through the states, it has lost its impact, while previously it was an effective agent in bringing about change and school improvement.

THE CRAFT OF TEACHING

Teacher training must be radically reorganized and realigned if it is ever to become compatible with the needs of modern youth and to successfully staff a broadly comprehensive high school. In schools properly using independent study there is a need for four types of teachers, all especially trained. The emerging roles of the teacher are as follows:

1. *The Lecturer:* This individual should be a skilled lecturer highly trained in the techniques of communication and the use of language. The training of "tellers" should center around techniques of presentation. In modern education, this methodology includes a great deal more than mere voice projection. The lecturer should be skilled in the use of educational technology, including the overhead projector, slide tapes, video tape recorders, and a host of audio-visual media.
2. *The Provocateur:* The provoker of learning should be a specialist in techniques of small group discussions. His job is to prod rather than to placate. He might well be called an exasperater as his role is to stimulate, excite, and inspire. In the process, he must badger, vex, taunt, and enrage—all in the interest of learning. The provocateur is, in effect, a highly trained devil's advocate. The function of the provocateur is to challenge and motivate students. His entire role is to organize and direct challenging discussions.
3. *The Preceptor:* The director of the Student Independent Study Program is often referred to as a tutor. The preceptor's role is certainly one of directing the tutorial. We prefer to think of the preceptor as more than a tutor—he is an associate in learning. From the teacher training standpoint, he should be a combination of counselor and teacher.
4. *The Technologist:* Up to the present, teacher training institutions have treated educational technology with scant courtesy. Emerging developments in the field of educational technology require highly trained operators for the new

hardware. The training of personnel suited to this activity must center around techniques for working with students as individuals.

PATTERNS OF INDEPENDENT STUDY

There are many kinds of independent study. This particular treatment deals exclusively with the two kinds which are most appropriate in the high school: (1) the educational contract in which a student contracts to do a specific amount of work outside the classroom, often in place of time in the classroom, and (2) independent study in which a student selects a topic for thorough study and research.

The Educational Contract

There is a distinct difference between these two approaches. The educational contract is an extension of classroom work and is an agreement to accomplish either the classroom work in the place of regular class attendance, or some phase of it in a unique or novel way, either on the student's own time or in the place of regular class attendance.

The idea of students contracting with teachers to accomplish a specified amount of learning outside the classroom, or even away from the school, is not a new one. Historically, the modern day educational contract owes its development to the Dalton plan of contract education which was developed by Helen Parkhurst in the early twenties at Dalton, Massachusetts.

Surprisingly the educational contract has been more widely used over the years in Holland than in the United States. The Dutch became so enthusiastic over the educational contract that when Mrs. Parkhurst visited Holland, she was received with great honor by the Burgomaster of Amsterdam. The most outstanding educational contract plan in Holland is the one used by the Dalton Lyceum, which was organized around the theories advocated by Mrs. Parkhurst. This secondary school has probably operated longer on the educational contract than any other institution.

The history of contracted education in the United States is that it was used extensively during the ensuing period following its development, but fell into disrepute largely because school staffs of that period could not adapt to the freedom which the contractural method gave to students.

The search for newer and better ways of educating boys and girls has now brought on a great revival of the contract. It is a clearly understood method of learning, and one which contributes significantly to the development of individual skills.

Contracts can be agreed upon for any given amount of work. The contract may be signed specifying a project, a particular unit or chapter of work, or even an entire course. The concept is a viable one and holds much potential for aiding the individual to learn how to learn on his own.

The Enabling Notion

By far the most exciting pattern of independent study is the comprehensive model, which allows any student to study independently any concept or body of knowledge in which he is interested and from which he feels that he can profit.

A major objective of the enabling notion is to help students become more objective and discriminating. Socrates' trenchant statement, "The unexamined life is not worth living," is especially appropriate here. Individual learners, unprotected against their own biases, can discover that life lacks coherence, purpose, and flavor unless they understand the issues and are seeking the truth.

Today's high school student will live in an era in which venturesome imagination and the capacity to organize large quantities of information are in great demand. In such a time, biases must be educated out! The individual must be able to achieve, in himself, a solid foundation for his opinions and actions. In such a time, the individual cannot be effective simply by assuming an unorthodox position.

Deciding upon ideals is a high personal activity. Furthermore, it is both difficult and confusing and fills the individual with uncertainty. Shakespeare said it well when he wrote, "This above all, to thine own self be true." Independent study, properly structured, helps the individual to examine his biases and become more dependent on his own resources, because he has developed personal standards.

In the past, the individual has been able to rely on family, community and church, but in modern society he is required to move so swiftly from one activity to another that he must possess a greater degree of self-reliance than individuals have required in the past. In such a setting biases must be treated and eliminated; independent study provides the vehicle by which this is best accomplished.

Recently I directed an International Seminar on the subject of "The Individual and the School" at Oxfordshire, England. The seminar concluded that the biggest problem facing schools in all countries today is the question of the nature of student independence and the development of techniques for encouraging the strengthening of this quality in students.

Principles of Independent Study

1. Independent study is a method of overcoming the limitations of the conventional school curriculum.
2. Independence in learning allows the student unlimited opportunities for expanding his personal knowledge about a subject.
3. The process of independent study allows the more able student to range ahead of his classmates.
4. Any student can go beyond the limits of the school's program of studies.
5. The individual's tempo for learning governs his progress.
6. Independent study motivates the individual student to learn how to learn.
7. It encourages the student to reach his own conclusions after he has explored a topic of interest to him as an individual.
8. The student acquires practice in selecting printed materials appropriate to his own style of learning.
9. The student can acquire sophisticated library research techniques.
10. It provides a platform for the student who has his own ideas and wants to share his ideas with other students and his teachers.
11. It helps the student become a producer, as well as a consumer, of learning.
12. Students are provided with an environment in which they can be creative.

13. Students develop individualized styles and approaches to learning.
14. It gives every student an opportunity to pursue a project or a research study in his own unique way.
15. It enables students to pursue advanced or creative topics at individualized rates of progress.
16. Students have an opportunity to work alone, with a teacher available for resource assistance.
17. The school curriculum satisfies the burgeoning trend in colleges for more independent study.

The gist of the matter is that the individual learner must be able to perform like a deep sea diver, moving freely up and down through the various strata of culture and opinion, lingering where it seems worthwhile to linger, and moving rapidly where it is appropriate to do so. Learning is dislocated from teaching and tempered to the style of the individual.

THE IMPORTANCE OF THE QUESTION

Philip Morrison, former professor of physics at Cornell, described the past attitude of teachers towards questions better than anyone else in a comment on his own education:

> We sat through 40 lectures; we were never allowed to ask any questions. One man once asked a question, whereupon the lecturer stopped, took off his glasses, wiped them, put them back on again, trembled a bit, and said in a very quiet voice, "This is a difficult course. There are many theorems to be introduced. If you ask questions we shall never get through." And after thirty seconds to let the vibration dampen, he began again.

If there are no questions there can be no answers, and the caliber of the question determines the quality of the answer. When students are searching for significant answers to well-posed questions, the process of independent study is greatly accelerated. Perhaps even more important than the search for answers, is the quest for questions. Posing significant questions is one of the most important functions of the student involved in independent study.

Reinhold Niebuhr once said, "I thought I had all the answers until I discovered that the questions to which I had the answers were not the important questions."

TRANSCENDENTAL KNOWING

The evidence is mounting that the process by which individuals make decisions can be learned. But decision making requires practice and plenty of it. Helping individuals to learn this process is rapidly becoming one of the major goals of education. All students should learn the elements of intuition and decision making. With reference to the decision-making component of independent study, intuition plays a significant role. The shrewd guess is a kind of talent which is receiving a great deal of attention. Student guessing should no longer be penalized. The way a person guesses his way around in this world has become increasingly important. The schools have, in the past, paid entirely too little attention to the process of guessing.

Jerome Bruner, the Harvard psychologist, more clearly than anyone else called for intuitive thinking to be a curriculum theme when he described "the nature of intuition as the intellectual technique of arriving at plausible but tentative formulations without going through the analytic steps." According to Bruner, "The shrewd guess, the fertile hypothesis, the courageous leap to a tentative conclusion—these are the most valuable coin of the thinker at work, whatever his line of work." This is a great gift which school youngsters must be taught to master.

The ability to perceive an outcome without going through the reasoning process is an important asset to any individual and has for too long been kept out of the learning process. Instinctive perception is a form of ideation which should be an integral part of each discipline. In essence, the schools should support all types of cognition, including the ability to perceive without going through any rational process.

THE COLLOQUIUM

Perhaps the most significant learning experience which a high school student can have is the experience of conducting a colloquium. This has made the colloquium a highly significant part of the independent study program.

The colloquium experience comes into play when this type of arrangement is used as a forum for exposing an independent study project to scrutiny and examination. The excitement of disclosing his research to a group of experts for examination adds another dimension to the thrill of discovery which comes into play when a student goes through the discovery process that is such a vital part of any independent study program.

The way the colloquium works is as follows: When the student selects this form of reporting, he and his preceptor work up a colloquium plan. Once the plan is drawn up, one of the student's major objectives in his independent study project is to prepare for the colloquium. What is contained in the colloquium plan? The time and place where the forum examination will be held, the names of the panel of scholars who will quiz the student, the number of people who will be invited, and a statement as to whether the colloquium will be open to all of the school or whether admission will be by invitation.

The most effective type of colloquium is one which has a panel of two to four scholars, a scholar for this activity being any person who is an expert in the field in which the independent study project took place, and an audience of approximately twenty seated in seminar style around the room. This arrangement accommodates the element of questions or criticism from the floor after the student has been orally questioned by his panel of scholars.

The use of the colloquium is highly recommended for most independent study projects. It is a lively learning situation in which everyone enjoys participating. The panel of scholars, who are usually community citizens with expertise in a particular field, often profess that they got as much out of the give-and-take situation as did the independent study student. Interested invitees are treated as seminar conferees and they also usually attest to an interesting experience in learning.

6

Patterns of Grouping in the
Comprehensive High School

The methods by which teaching and learning are transacted in the new curricula of the comprehensive high school are emerging both loudly and clearly. Unfortunately this clarity has not penetrated the clouds of confusion which overhang teacher training institutions. These organizations have turned pedagogy, which should be a very exciting happening, into a pedantic discipline utterly devoid of elan. If one listens to the renunciations of the trainees of teacher training institutions, pedagogy has indeed become a dismal science.

Teacher training institutions should be engaged in a massive effort to assure that every prospective teacher receives extensive training in the area of group dynamics. No teacher should be certified for a certificate unless he is intimately acquainted with the skills of directing learning in the small group. Every teacher both new and old must be able to understand the small group rationale and be comfortable with its application. Maximum learning takes place when an individual or group breaks the umbilical cord of dependence on the teacher and assumes the responsibility for learning. This happening occurs most frequently in the small group.

The most viable training which a teacher can obtain is a solid grounding in the skills and techniques of organizing, developing, and operating small groups for the purpose of learning.

The most obvious problem of teaching and learning within the high school itself is the traditional grouping of students into class-rooms of thirty. This is not a teachable group. The difficulty with breaking up this pattern centers around the fact that the schools are built with strings of classrooms in a row, each one containing 750 square feet. These rooms are squared so that they will neatly accommodate five rows of desks with six to a row. The result is that the school has a built-in polarization of thirty students to a class. From an administrative point of view each youngster can be easily slotted and re-slotted as the occasion demands.

In order to make learning a more personal happening, this barrier of self-containment must be overcome. It is essential that much of the individual's learning time be spent in a much smaller group. For instructional activities, the class can, and should, be sub-divided into smaller groups.

The new curriculum of the comprehensive high school places a great deal more emphasis on affective learning than have the curricula of the past. The past practice of concentrating only on the cognitive must give way to a balance between the affective and the cognitive. Affective learning is best accomplished in small groups; consequently they are beginning to play a vital role in the new goals and purposes of the secondary school.

The small group as a process is being viewed with increasing importance by a growing number of professions. Psychiatrists are using the small group as a means of providing therapy for emotionally disturbed people through a "here and now" approach which they now consider more practical than the traditional technique of probing into the patient's past. Psychologists are employing the small group process in sensitivity training sessions designed to give the individual more "self-insight" into his problems. Sociologists contend that the small group is the best method to use in "teaching people to care about other people." Personnel managers are increasingly utilizing the version of the small group technique called T-grouping for the purpose of "minimizing destructive competition between departments within the company." And, for the past decade, educators have been juggling conventionally large school groups into small groups in an effort to accommodate more efficient teaching and learning.

The small group is seen by educators as the best methodology for achieving either of two objectives:

(1) The involvement of students in a confrontation through the use of encounter group techniques, frequently in an attempt to bring about racial understanding.

(2) A way of increasing student involvement in the learning process.

This chapter is devoted entirely to the notion of *learning* in the small group and is an attempt to explore the many nuances of learning which are possible in the small group situation.

THE TAXONOMY OF EDUCATIONAL OBJECTIVES

The implications for learning in the small group are most effectively viewed when focused against the taxonomy of educational objectives as organized by Benjamin S. Bloom. Bloom defined types of educational behavior ranging from simple to complex in order of difficulty. He singled out the mere acquisition of knowledge as the simplest form of behavior, and evaluation the most complex. Bloom's taxonomy of learning behaviors, in ascending order of complexities, is as follows:

1.00 Knowledge
2.00 Comprehension
3.00 Application
4.00 Analysis
5.00 Synthesis
6.00 Evaluation

The small group provides the setting, dynamics, and intellectual stimulation for the attainment of the more complex of Bloom's objectives. When effectively performed, the activities of the small group permit more favorable learning than is possible in the classroom.

THE PURPOSE

Too often, the small group is organized for the purpose of supporting a formal presentation. This treatment is one of the weaker uses of the technique. Small group learning is an end in itself, and can be generated much more effectively than following a lecture with the discussion based on controversial points in the lecture.

In the more productive groups, deliberation rather than discussion takes place. Group deliberation, aimed at cooperative problem solving or resolution of a conflict through reflective thinking, is a highly complex learning behavior. The aim of the small group is to provide students with the vehicle by which they can attain the highest behavioral objectives.

In addition to intensified learning opportunities there are a number of other important learnings which are derived from participation in the small group. These include the development of a penchant for active listening and the ability to generate ideas from hitchhiking on another person's comments.

The small group, more than any other learning arrangement, provides interaction, confronts students with the dynamics of human behavior, and generates intense involvement with the learning situation.

The gist of the matter is that the activities of the learning group are concerned almost entirely with either one or more, or a combination of the behaviors of analysis, synthesis and evaluation. In essence, Bloom's most complex behaviors and the ones most difficult to achieve are best attained in the various versions of the small group.

SIZE OF THE LEARNING SMALL GROUP

The number of persons in a small group varies according to (1) the activity, and (2) the purpose for which the group is formed. Sociologists, who should know all there is to know about grouping, disagree on how many people constitute a group, but we like the definition put forth by one sociologist that:

> Two persons are a group and even one person is a group
> if he is interacting, from memory, with another person.

Educators, like sociologists, are at odds over the question: What is the most appropriate number for a small group? Since educators must cope with large numbers of students, they universally consider from ten to fifteen students as a desirable number for a small group and most pedagogs write about this number in a small group. This is entirely too many students for interaction, and the small group, as described in this chapter, constitutes no fewer than five and no more than eight students. Less than five is usually too few a number and the product of a group this small tends to resemble committee work. More than eight in a group is too many, and the effort of eight or more simulates that of a class more than that of a small group. While from five to eight is a good rule of thumb, there are exceptions which require even smaller groups. There are none which would warrant more persons to a group. A good exception of fewer than five members is the investigative group which must be more of a mini-group because of the necessity for constant contact between members for the purpose of checking and cross-checking data.

There are many kinds of small learning groups, but some are much more valuable than others in providing high quality instruction. It is now well established that the techniques of small group learning are highly effective for (1) enhancing motivation to learn, (2) developing positive attitudes toward later use of course material, and (3) improving problem-solving skills.

THE SMALL GROUP AS A COMPONENT

The initial prominence of the small group in the learning process can be attributed to the team teaching movement of the early sixties. The principles of this movement conceived of learning taking place in large groups, small groups, and independent study, with roughly equal time devoted to each activity. By the same token, the small group has long been a component in the conventional class, always easy to organize by merely sub-dividing the class. The problem here has been the lack of skill on the part of the teacher in coping with the small group operation. Contrary to what many teachers think, the small group exercise is a highly complicated process. Too many teachers think that it is no more than dividing the students into groups and giving them a problem to discuss. When this is all that is done, the teacher may as well keep them in the traditional class. Any learning is strictly accidental and the opportunity for good learning experiences has been left strictly to chance. There are many skills which must be mastered if the small group is to be productive.

THE BLOOM IS OFF THE GROSS

The contribution of the team teaching movement to the use of small group learning in schools should be recognized. Team teaching as a major movement in secondary education dates back no further than 1956. It was developed largely by J. Lloyd Trump as a plan for changing the teacher's role. Dr. Trump urged that student learning be organized so that students would be able to spend 40% of their time in large group instruction, 40% in independent study, and 20% in small group discussion. Unfortunately, the time for gross learning in the large group was excessive.

The team teaching movement failed because of the over-emphasis on the component of large group instruction. Teachers generally approached team teaching by keeping ninety or more students in large group situations too much of the time. In these sessions, the teachers took turns lecturing, showed a film, or had the youngsters view educational television. The classes were so dull and the learning so passive that the movement was abandoned as a high school innovation.

It is conceivable that the movement would have been successful had the emphasis been placed upon small group learning and independent study, rather than on large group instruction. Listening, or viewing, which are the two things that happen in large group instruction, are both passive activities and should occupy no more than 10% of the student's time. Students must be much more actively engaged in the learning process, if learning is to be accomplished. The small group can achieve a much higher degree of problem solving than is possible in a lecture.

For high schools who still wish to try out team teaching I recommend a revision of the Trump formula so that the time is roughly allocated as follows:

> 10% of the time in large group activities
> 45% of the time in small group learning
> 45% of the time in independent study

The time in small group learning and independent study is variable. Time spent in the large group is almost inflexible. It can vary downward but not upward. Never should it exceed 10% of the student's time. Passive sitting and listening or viewing must be minimized in the large group setting. These functions can be achieved just as well in private and with more interaction. Gross learning in large group settings has little place in the new curricula of the high school.

THE RATIONALE

Everyone talks about the individualization of instruction, but very few educators do anything about it. The best understood methods for individualization instruction are programmed learning books, unipaks, and computer assisted learning. My position on this matter is that totally individualized instruction is neither essential nor feasible. In fact, it is probably not even desirable. What is fitting, expedient, and proper is an intensive learning experience for the individual.

This intensive learning occurs best in a collectivity of six students sitting with a teacher where they can have close contact with his knowledge and insights, or sitting with their peers where they have the opportunity to compare, dissent, harmonize, analyze and evaluate.

In a large group, such as the conventional class of thirty, or even a collectivity of fifteen, learning remains too passive and many individuals remain uncommitted to the matter at hand. With no more than five or six to the group, there is a natural pressure for high involvement and it is nearly impossible to remain uncommitted.

One of the significant happenings of the collectivity of six is that it provides a supportive climate and breaks down resistance to learning. The process of changing one's attitudes, opinions and thought patterns is a difficult one, but when it is done in conjunction with the changing of others, it becomes a natural happening. Intensive involvement in small group activity reduces defensiveness and anxiety while helping the individual to become more mature at the same time. A few of the functions of the cohesive group which support readiness for learning are as follows:[6]

1. Expectations among members that everyone will learn.
2. Acceptance that learning and change are desirable and not a mark of previous inadequacy.
3. Recognition that individuals may make mistakes but, since all are learning, errors will not be punished by the group or other members.
4. Realistic levels of aspiration for the group and for all members in terms of new learnings to be achieved.

The collectivity of six has proven to be highly productive, whether the learners are talented, recalcitrant, experienced or inexperienced. This type of learning situation also is more appropriate to a "mix" of the fast and slow than any other type of grouping.

SUB-GROUPING

Surviving from the team teaching plan is the notion of sub-grouping the class for discussion. The advantage of smaller sub-groups is that a group of five or six students is more task oriented than a class of thirty. The small group feels more of a compulsion to get on with the job to be done than does the conventional class because each person in the group is more involved than when in the larger setting.

The effective small group is one which gets on with its job without delay and with relative efficiency. It accomplishes this with a degree of grace and productivity.

The small group expert Stephen M. Corey describes the following characteristics of the productive small group once the large class has been broken down:[7]

1. The task of the group is clear and accepted as important by all members.
2. The members of the group feel free to express themselves—not afraid.

---

[6] Technical Report 70-3, *Theory and State of the Art of Small-Group Methods of Instruction,* prepared for Office, Chief of Research and Development Dept. of the Army, Ft. Benning, Ga., March 1970.
[7] Letter to the author.

3. Responsibilities involved in getting the job done are differentiated and shared.
4. Actions to be taken are made explicit and personnel to take them are designated.
5. Good communication skills are practiced (listening, checking for clarity, disciplined responding, sticking to the point).
6. The way the group is going about its task is examined when progress is blocked.

Dr. Corey lists the following as examples of Behavioral Objectives which can be achieved in the sub-class small group:[8]

1. After hearing a group member speak, is able to repeat, tersely, the gist of what he has said. This is behavior bearing centrally on the LISTENING dimension.
2. During group discussion perceives and is able to signal his perception of statements wide of the theme, whatever it may be. This behavior represents the capability to stick to the issue, or better, perceive when this isn't done by someone else.
3. Perceive the need for skillful timing, and provide summaries.
4. Perceive the need for, and test effectively for, group consensus.
5. Perceive the need for and provide or solicit information and/or opinion.
6. Perceive the need for and provide clarification.
7. Differentiate among the several major dimensions of productive group work and help the group when blocked.

Dr. Corey has also established the necessary essential task-centered roles for productive groups. He feels that before the group can get on with its task someone in the group must take on certain roles at appropriate times and fulfill some necessary functions. The first class of roles is for the group to concentrate on what he calls the "out there" task.

TASK-CENTERED ROLES

1. Requests clarification
2. Summarizes

---

[8] Ibid.

3. Proposes actions
4. Tests for consensus
5. Solicits needed information and/or opinions
6. Provides needed information and/or opinions
7. Examines group processes

Corey's other roles which he feels are the responsibility of all group members are:

1. Gives encouragement
2. Reflects own and group's feelings
3. Sets standards and norms for group
4. Keeps communication channels open
5. Reconciles and harmonizes
6. Relieves tensions—jokes, etc.

There are a number of types of specific groups but the most widely used is the discussion group. For this reason, this is discussed in depth.

THE DISCUSSION GROUP

The discussion group should consist of at least five but not more than six members. The ideal size for discussion purposes is a six-member group. The key to success in this group is threefold:

1. Good preparation by the group members.
2. A thorough understanding by the group members of the underlying roles they are expected to play.
3. Well-stated objectives.

The optimum time for this activity can be as long as one class period or a portion thereof, depending upon the material to be discussed and the preparation of group members. The teacher serves as a consultant only in the discussion group and his role is made more provocative if he does not give direct answers but responds to a question with a question.

In planning the use of discussion groups, it is important that the groups not be too loosely structured. Very often teachers put discussion groups together without the group members being adequately prepared for either the discussion or the process.

In order to ensure success, the teacher should (1) take steps to make certain that the students are well prepared on the topic to be discussed, and (2) give each group member an underlying responsibility for representing a particular point of view. The points of view may vary with the subject matter but following are several suggested personifications:

Moderator	Harmonizer
Objectivator	Reporter
Provocateur	Evaluator

When each group member personifies a point of view, group reaction and results are much more provocative and students tend to become more intimately involved in the work of the group.

The discussion mode is most often used in mini-courses, social studies, the humanities, and literature courses but it can be adapted to any subject area. This is a useful technique following a project in independent study.

The aforementioned commonly used points of view and the responsibilities of each are as follows:

MODERATOR: This group member has the responsibility for seeing that each member of the group has an opportunity to participate in an orderly fashion. He encourages participation from the shyer members of the group. He is not required to undertake but is free to enter the discussion and take sides just like any other group member.

OBJECTIVATOR: The objectivator affirms the objectives of the activity and makes every effort to keep the group pointed towards the group goal. From time to time he restates the objectives and in so doing keeps the group centered on its goals.

PROVOCATEUR/DISSENTER: The provocateur/dissenter's role as defined by students who have represented this point of view is to "toss in those little nifties or suggest little upsetting things which throw the group off balance." Perhaps a better definition of this role is that of "devil's advocate."

RECORDER/REPORTER: The recorder/reporter takes notes on the major points brought out and discussed in the small group. He then must interpret or report to other groups, reporters from other groups, or the class, depending upon the arrangements.

HARMONIZER: The harmonizer strives to keep harmony in the group. He intercedes when one or more members become argumentative and endeavors to keep the group functioning on an even keel.

EVALUATOR: The evaluator assesses the performance of the group by analyzing the following happenings:

1. Did all members of the group participate on near-equal basis or was domination evident?
2. Was there reasonably equal participation by both sexes or did one sex tend to dominate?
3. Were group members considerate of one another?
4. Were group members good listeners?

THE DEADLOCK CONCEPT

Strictly from the point of view of participation the optimum size for the small group discussion is five members. However, it should be pointed out that group deadlock on an issue is not possible when a group is composed of an odd number of members. Since the deadlock and subsequent conflict resolution constitute a significant learning experience, when all of the subtleties are taken into consideration the optimum size for the discussion group is six members.

When students go through the process of resolving a conflict in which they have been deadlocked, the learning dividends are enormous. They gain remarkable new insights into the value of compromise which cannot be learned in any other way. The teacher who is deeply sensitive to group dynamics always arranges situations in which a deadlock will develop.

After students have experienced several stalemates where resolution seemed impossible, and worked through solutions, they show tremendous growth in maturity. The resolution of an impasse can be a very exciting happening in learning.

THE INVESTIGATIVE GROUP

This group is ordinarily smaller than the five- to eight-member learning group and consists usually of three, but seldom more than four, members. Since the very nature of an investigation requires close coordination, the group must of necessity be kept small if the investigative activities are going to be subjected to the processes of analysis, synthesis, and evaluation.

The investigative group is usually project oriented and frequently works together for the entire semester or longer. Science teachers in high school report satisfactory results from investigative groups working as long as two years together.

The plan of laboratory investigation that is most popular among both students and teachers was developed by the National Science Foundation:

> No research investigation of any kind can be carried on without approval of the laboratory director. Approval requires that a complete, quantitative, step-by-step procedure be submitted.

> The rationale and complete references to the literature should be fully described for each step in the procedure as follows:

Example:

	Rationale	*Reference*
1) EMB agar (100ml.) to be sterilized at 15 lbs. for 15 minutes.	This pressure and the resulting temperature will kill all bacteria and their spores	Doe, John, *Journal of Molecular Biology,* 96, 206 (1965)

Other important kinds of specific type small groups are as follows:

> Brainstorming Group
> Heuristic Group
> Tutorial Group
> Creative Talk Group
> Socratic-Analysis   Group

Assigned-Roles Group
Investigative Group

EVALUATION

Following every small group exercise there should be an evaluation. This assessment of performance and success can take one
of two forms. The most often used type is for one member of
the group to evaluate the participation of other members and the
overall performance of the group. This is by far the best method
as it involves comments from the other members and spices up
the interest. Most groups look forward to the evaluation.

In order to keep groups concentrating on their efficiency and
productivity, the evaluation should be varied, and occasionally
individuals should respond with a written evaluation. Perhaps the
best individual assessment was compiled by the National Congress
of Parents and Teachers from a number developed by the Center
for the Study of Liberal Education for Adults, which at the time
of the development was directed by Mr. A. A. Liveright.

ASSESSMENT OF PERFORMANCE[9]

1. To what extent did the group concentrate its efforts on the
   discussion task?

   ____were at work most of the time
   ____worked but spent some time talking about other things
   ____spent a good deal of time on other things

2. If there were times when the group did not work well,
   what may have been the reason?

   ____were quibbling over irrelevancies
   ____were being sociable, joking, et cetera
   ____were off on irrelevant personal experiences
   ____were frustrated

3. Most of the talking was done by

   ____group as a whole
   ____a few members
   ____the leader

---

[9] *When Parents Study Their Job Techniques,* PTA discussion groups, National Congress of Parents and Teachers, 700 N. Rush St., Chicago, Ill., pp. 53–55.

4. So far as guiding the discussion is concerned, the leader

_____shared guidance with the group
_____managed it mostly himself
_____provided no guidance

5. Differing points of view were

_____acknowledged and considered impartially
_____acknowledged but not considered objectively
_____neither acknowledged nor considered

6. Members participated in ways which helped make the discussion productive

_____by encouraging other members to contribute
_____by calling attention to points of agreement or disagreement
_____by summarizing
_____by attempting to clarify
_____by introducing relevant new points for consideration
_____by bringing the group back to the subject
_____by trying to resolve conflict

7. The goals of the discussion were

_____clearly set by the leader
_____developed by the leader and members of the group
_____indefinite and uncertain

8. The general climate during the discussion was

_____rather tense, people not at ease
_____quite relaxed, people quite at ease
_____fairly relaxed
_____such that few people were stimulated to participate
_____such that participation and involvement came naturally and generally

9. Members paid attention to what others were saying

_____always
_____frequently
_____sometimes
_____rarely
_____never

10. Members understood one another

_____very well

_____fairly well
_____very little
_____not at all

11. Attempts were made to clarify ideas and thinking by probing for reasons behind opinions

_____always
_____frequently
_____sometimes
_____rarely
_____never
_____by members
_____by leader

12. Evidence used to support opinions was evaluated for soundness

_____always
_____frequently
_____sometimes
_____rarely
_____never

PRODUCTS OF THE SMALL GROUP

An essential element of the small group process is the identification in the beginning of the outcome which is expected. This outcome most often assumes the form of an oral report. Next in order of frequency is a written report.

The most desirable outcome, and one which the author feels strongly about, is a worthwhile audio or visual report using the media of the cassette tape or, for the more complex conclusions, the cassette geared to slides, taking the form of a slide tape. There is much to be said for these media. First, if a student uses the cassette, he is forced to conceptualize or editorialize his report. This tends to make for a crisper and more sophisticated approach toward the achievement of his objectives. The slide tape requires even greater conceptualization and puts the student through both the synthesis and the evaluative processes. This requires more conceptualization than any other type of report including a film. The slide tape requires analysis, synthesis and evaluation of not only the findings, but also the way the report is put together. The group must first conceptualize in film through slides and then plan and execute the narration. Many teachers are now requiring that appropriate music be used to accompany the slide-tape.

THE DILEMMA

The most serious problem confronting the use of the small group process is the lack of training for teachers either before assuming their duties as teachers, or as part of their in-service training subsequent to their employment. It is indeed unfortunate that the teacher training institutions are not preparing teachers to use the small group process. Instead they continue "fitting teachers for an unfitted fitness." And the employing school systems are managing to keep them unfit by the lack of viable in-service training in small group work. Some trainers contend that the biggest obstacle to widespread use of the small group process with teaching and learning is what they refer to as "the dependency issue." This exists because the teachers want the youngsters to be dependent upon them in the learning process.

When the small group is used, the picture is radically changed and the students carry the ball in the learning process with very little dependence upon the teacher.

SUMMARY

Since their beginnings, the schools have concentrated only on cognitive skills. Everything happening in the schools has been geared to the act of knowing or thinking.

Desegregation and the pressure for integration, coupled with the newly won student freedom, are changing the emphasis from the intellectual to a balance between thinking skills and happenings, which involve the feelings or emotions of individuals. This latter is generally referred to as affective learning.

In the new comprehensive curriculum there should be an equal emphasis on the cognitive and the affective. This change in direction brings into prominence the potential of the small group. It is a superb technique for teaching youngsters to use affective skills.

Extensive new experience with small group activity indicates that the best sized group is a collectivity of six. This is just the right number to allow maximum participation. When the group is smaller than five it resembles a committee. If it is larger than eight it begins to resemble a class. In support of this notion a mathematics formula has been developed which effectively illustrates this point. This formula is as follows:

> The number of persons in the group minus one times the number of persons in the group equals the number of interactions.

$$NP - 1 \times NP = \text{Number of interactions}$$

For example, in a group of six there is a possibility of 30 interactions. The formula would be applied as follows:

$$NP - 1 \times NP = \text{Number of interactions}$$
$$6 - 1 \times 6 = 30$$

Note that even in a small group of only six there is a potential of 30 personal relationships, which is approaching the maximum number which an individual can handle effectively.

In summary, the use of the small group is emerging as one of the most effective of strategies for teaching and learning. The beauty of this innovation is that it does not require the approval of the school board, the superintendent, or even the principal. It is a strategy within the teacher's domain.

7

The Vocational Program in the Comprehensive High School

Recently, the U. S. Commissioner of Education called for radical changes in secondary education. He urged that the "abomination known as general education be abolished and replaced with contemporary 'career education' in a comprehensive school." He further proposed a "universal goal that every high school student graduate with a salable skill." If the schools are to come even close to Commissioner Marland's goal, then vocational education must be contracted out of the school. By contracting with community businesses as the training agencies, the schools can both expand and improve occupational education in one fell swoop. Providing the necessary physical facilities at the school would run into billions of dollars. This would also be a rank duplication of facilities which already exist in the community. More effective programs can be developed in true on the job situations than simulated vocational programs housed within the school.

In the comprehensive high school as conceived by Dr. Conant, the school should contain within its walls several shops and laboratories for vocational work. In the comprehensive high school as I conceive it, the school should offer unlimited occupational opportunities, but avoid the expense of having any of this type of activity going on at the school. How is this accomplished? Through contracting all vocational programs out among business or industrial organizations within the community. This provides not only a multitude of vocational opportunities, but also an in-depth exposure which fits in with the notion that the community should be an extension of the high school and all of its resources available for the learning opportunities of young people.

IMPROVING THE IMAGE

There is no question but what the past image of vocational education has been a poor one. The program has been a dumping ground for recalcitrant students not interested in schooling. Principals have taken the attitude that problem students are less conspicuous in vocational shops than anywhere else in the school. William Devonald, Editor of *News Magazine,* a publication of the New Jersey Vocational and Arts Educational Association, pinpointed this problem in an editorial in the November 1970 issue:

> Vocational education began its development in many places with makeshift facilities, used equipment and "second-class" students. In some ways it has never recovered from its humble beginnings. Not because the leadership didn't try, but because a lot of things were not going for its progress or advancement. Vocational education is still accepted by many people as something good for other people's children.

The time has now come for vocational or occupational education to develop and adopt first-class programs in order that its students may be second to none, in either the concept of self-respect or potential earning power.

PERFORMANCE CONTRACTING

The greatest promise for vastly improved vocational education can be found in the concept of performance contracting. This development offers a rubric for extensively improving occupational training. An analysis of the performance contract and its potential for vocational education is highly relevant. The performance contract is an agreement between a school board and a private group to increase the achievement of a group of students in a specified area of learning. This opens the door to a new kind of occupational education as community businesses take over the training of high school youth in a multitude of occupations and trades. The school board can contract for whatever degree of performance it wants, but a basic tenet of the performance contract is that if there is no increase in achievement level, no fee will be paid. If there is a greater-than-anticipated increase, a higher fee will be paid. The party which contracts to perform is usually a business group and the contract is hitched to increased achievement. Payment, based on achievement, is like profit and loss. It is language which the business world understands.

Credit for advancing and developing the concept of performance contracting with payment based upon student achievement goes to Charles Blaske of Education Turnkey Systems. While a graduate student at Harvard in 1964–65, Blashke developed an important paper on this subject; he crystalized the idea further during a tour of duty with Secretary MacNamara's office. It was Blashke who wrote the proposal and masterminded the famous Texarkana project which was the first major performance contract.

Performance contracting as an innovation is a managerial tool for changing schools. It is a method by which the schools can be held accountable and school reform can be managed. Furthermore, the performance contract is the only proven method that complies with the White House doctrine of accountability which states that the schools must be more accountable if they are to receive additional federal funds.

In his message to Congress on March 3, 1970, President Nixon expressed the following principles of accountability:

> We must stop pretending that we understand the mystery of the learning process, or that we are significantly applying science and technology to the techniques of teaching. . . .
>
> When educators, school boards and government officials alike admit that we have a great deal to learn about the way we teach, we will begin to climb the up staircase toward genuine reform. . . .
>
> What makes a "good" school? The old answer was a school that maintained high standards of plant and equip-

ment; that had a reasonable number of children per class-room; whose teachers had good college and often graduate training; a school that kept up to date with new curriculum developments, and was alert to new techniques in instruction. This was a fair enough definition so long as it was assumed that there was a direct connection between these "school characteristics" and the actual amount of learning that takes place in a school. . . .

Unfortunately, it is simply not possible to make any confident deduction from school characteristics as to what will be happening to the children in any particular school. Fine new buildings alone do not predict high achievement. Pupil-teacher ratios may not make as much difference as we used to think. Expensive equipment may not make as much difference as its salesmen would have us believe. . . .

From these considerations we derive another new concept: *accountability*. School administrators and school teachers alike are responsible for their performance, and it is in their interest as well as in the interests of their pupils that they be held accountable. Success should be measured not by some fixed national norm, but rather by the results achieved in relation to the actual situation of the particular school and the particular set of pupils.

For years the fear of "national standards" has been one of the bugaboos of education. There has never been any serious effort to impose national standards on educational programs, and if we act wisely in this generation we can be reasonably confident that no such effort will arise in future generations. The problem is that in opposing some mythical threat of "national standards" what we have too often been doing is avoiding accountability for our own local performance. We have, as a nation, too long avoided thinking of the *productivity* of schools. . . .[10]

The schools have generally refused to be held accountable for learning while the performance contract relates student learning and performance to payment for the teaching service rendered.

[10] *Message on Education Reform,* Richard Nixon's address to the Congress of the United States, March 3, 1970.

Both of the national teacher organizations, the N.E.A. and the A.F.T., are in vigorous opposition to the performance contract. Neither have they accepted the notion that teachers must be held more accountable. On the other hand the American Management Association recently held a seminar dealing with "how the advent of performance contracting as an alternative instructional system will affect existing school systems."

This book takes the position that the American Management Association's prognostication is more realistic than the opposition of the teacher unions. Conventional schooling is in serious trouble and the search is on for alternate systems of education.

The unfortunate part of the dilemma is that, to date, the performance contractors have concentrated on the wrong part of the curricula. Instead of developing new programs for vocational education, which is a natural area of business, the concentration has been largely on the teaching of reading. This matter is almost an absurdity, but the teaching of reading has reached such a debacle that business has jumped into a void.

THE NEW VOCATIONAL CURRICULA

The conventional vocational education program which exists in most comprehensive high schools is in a serious state of intellectual disrepair. It is little better in the strictly vocational schools which offer nothing but vocational work. What is wrong? Everything that is being done. For the purpose of analyzing the ills of vocational education an examination of the program as it exists in traditional comprehensive high schools is important.

The conventional program houses within the walls of the comprehensive school from three to nine vocational programs, with the average being five or six. The most frequently offered program is training in auto mechanics. Since this occupation is almost the first one instituted when a school undertakes comprehensiveness, it has been selected as a microcosm of the vocational education program to be examined in depth.

A first-class well-equipped shop costs approximately $250,000. The instructor is an auto mechanic with six years of experience on the job and a couple of courses in teacher training. He is paid $10,000 a year. He teaches approximately 16 students in two- or three-hour blocks of time and usually handles about thirty-two students during the day. If the school decides to offer automobile body work, it needs to build and equip another $250,000 shop and employ another instructor.

Many of the youngsters enrolled in school-housed auto mechanics classes are not seriously interested in auto mechanics as an occupation. They are there because they like "fooling around with cars" and want to escape the deadly boredom of the classroom. Follow-up studies of what happens to these students upon graduation is a carefully guarded vocational secret. The establishment dares not reveal the results of follow-up studies which are made annually. Actually, no more than three or four percent of the students who participate in the program go into auto mechanics work after graduation from high school.

Where does the shop get cars to repair? Usually it cannot take in work off the street for a number of reasons. For example, it can only charge small fees because of its trainee labor and the fact that the program is tax supported. If it does take in work off the street the local automobile dealers protest; consequently, the source of the work in the school shop is limited to the following: (1) an auto engine donated by one of the big three auto makers; (2) junked cars which are bought as junk; (3) students' and teachers' cars. Because of these factors, there is built into the school auto mechanics shop a highly artificial situation when it is compared to an auto repair business serving the general public.

By comparison, examine the difference in the quality of a performance contracted program in auto mechanics. First, there is no expensive capital outlay for the construction and equipping of a school housed shop. Second, the school does not have to maintain and upkeep a shop with regular expenditures for replacement of broken tools, machines, etc. Third, when students are working or apprenticing in a real shop, they have access to a number of instructors who are specialized in many aspects of auto repair. Fourth, the learning situation is real.

The schools should not attempt to duplicate training which can be more efficiently and economically carried on in more realistic situations. What the schools have been doing in vocational education is duplicating business facilities in the community, and at tremendous cost. To continue this is absurd. An on-the-job trainee gains enormous insight into the occupation, an insight which has many subtleties that he misses in the simulation of the high school shop.

Under the concept of the new philosophy of using the community and its resources as curriculum support, all the school has to do is to employ a knowledgeable person in the field of vocational work to oversee the program. He arranges the placement of serious students in shops, sets up the performance contract with the shop, and approves payment to the contractor at intervals when the student has acquired certain marketable skills. This individual is paid approximately the same salary as the erstwhile auto mechanic instructor and the school pays a modest training fee for each student. The expense of constructing and maintaining large shops which are duplicates of existing community shops is saved to the taxpayer.

It is ridiculous to continue the traditional archaic vocational education program at schools when students can be placed in viable learning situations on the job in the community work area of the curricula.

The beauty of this new program is that the new comprehensive high school is not limited to whatever shops the school system can afford to have built. A student can enter any vocation which is available in his community. For example, no high school can afford a program so varied that it would include watchmaking. Yet, when the school contracts its vocational training, if there are only one or two students who are interested in this particular occupation, training can easily be arranged with a local jeweler who has a watch repair shop.

One of the more enlightened of the vocational educators is Dr. John Struck, Director of Vocational Education for the Pennsylvania Department of Education. In a recent article on the topic of contracting training outside of the school, Dr. Struck described the new curricula as follows:

> In the next decade greater emphasis will be placed on local resources. Businessmen and industrial people are anxious to help the public schools. Bankers, lawyers, and insurance men are delighted to be asked to meet with high school groups or to teach a short course in their special area. The

talents of these people are impossible to duplicate in the faculty of high schools.

Drawn out courses must be shortened. Public schools insist that courses must last a full year. Is it impossible for public schools to offer a three-month course to secondary school students? We should have short courses of many varieties and be prepared to offer them as they are needed. Private schools can take a student at any day in the year. Through individual teaching methods, they can give him anything he wants. We in public education have got to do this.

Cooperative education programs will be expanded. Shops and labs are hampered in the school system. Our work force is now splintered into a thousand different occupations. It would be impossible for schools to offer practical laboratories for every occupation. What do we do if a student wants to learn watchmaking?

The only answer is a cooperative program where the student goes out and works in such a business, side by side with the expert. Business and industrial people are most willing to do this type of training. By expanding cooperative programs we will provide more realistic, well-rounded education.

We will initiate intensive courses for our youth who are out of school. Few of our public schools do much for the boy or girl who dropped out, was pushed out, or even graduated. Thousands of able young men and women who are not going to college for one reason or another have no skills to get a job. Our public schools feel their responsibility to youths ends once they are out of school.

Vocational education is an integral part of all education. Consequently, education in the future must be concerned with all capacities of an individual.[11]

As Dr. Struck points out so forcefully, the public schools have shown no interest in either those who have dropped out of school,

11 *Pennsylvania Education*, July–August 1970, p. 26. Published by the Pennsylvania Department of Education, Harrisburg, Pa.

though still of school age, nor in those slightly over school age who are in need of the school's services. In the new curriculum, the school must accommodate and make welcome not only those two groups, but also any person of any age in the community who needs the school's services. This is especially true in the field of occupational information or training.

The factors which hinder the schools in reaching this group that must be overcome are:

1. Incompetent occupational counseling.
2. Lack of insight on the part of educators and school board members into the potential of occupational training through performance contracting.
3. Fear of change on the part of educators long used to the status quo.
4. A general lack of concern among teachers who are unappreciative of the importance of occupational training.

Throughout the country there is an ever increasing reluctance on the part of taxpayers to support schools. This is a result of the disenchantment which is abroad in the land over high school programs. Once the high school becomes truly comprehensive, it embraces its responsibility for training anyone with an educational need, either academic or occupational. This happening will result in far greater support for the schools by the local community. When the community becomes involved and functions as an extension of the school, its attitude toward support alters greatly.

THE DEBACLE OF VOCATIONAL EDUCATION

The debacle of vocational education is clearly seen when one examines (1) the cost, and (2) the product. According to the *American Vocational Journal,* the official publication of the American Vocational Association: "More than 1.8 billion dollars from the Federal, State and local sources were expended for vocational education programs during fiscal year 1970." If this cost estimate is correct, and one must assume that it is, then the expenditure for 1971 is well over two billion dollars.

The tragedy is that very few graduates from vocational school programs are equipped with job-entry skills. In a recent speech on the topic of students being equipped with job-entry skills. Representative Edwin B. Forsythe of New Jersey, one of the nation's more enlightened congressmen, pinpointed the debacle:

> I could recite statistics to show just how few Americans on the high school level really obtain any vocational education across this country. But, suffice it to say that of the high school students who do receive some vocational education training, I doubt if as many as one in five graduate with entry-level skills in any occupation.

ELEMENTARY SCHOOL VOCATIONAL EDUCATION

There is much talk abroad in the land about extending vocational education down into the elementary school. Millions of dollars have already been spent developing and widening programs in the junior high school. If what is happening in the junior high school is an indication of what the elementary school program will be like, then may heaven forbid. In connection with the research for this book I visited a number of industrial arts classes in a widely scattered group of junior high schools. To my consternation, the most frequent happening in these shops was the making of bread boards. Why bread boards? Probably because this is the easiest thing to make. It apparently never occurred to the industrial arts teachers that the bread comes sliced these days. My only comment is that if this is vocational education in the junior high school, and it definitely is, then may heaven help us if we extend it downward into the elementary schools!

COLLEGE IS NOT THE ANSWER

The number of high school students who go on to college, even in the states with the best high school education, averages well below 50%. Therefore, for at least half of our students, the responsibility of the high school is to prepare them for the world of work.

Although there has been a greatly increased emphasis on college education, with the federal government sponsoring programs almost aimlessly in their effort to take care of minority groups, college for all is not the answer. Everybody does not need a college education, nor does everybody want one. It is abundantly clear that everyone cannot make it in college, yet the attitude and programs of the federal government have been heavily weighted in this direction. They must now be turned around and put in balance with vocational training.

ANOTHER APPROACH

There is no question but what the best vocational schools in the world are located in Holland. In preparation for this study, I visited vocational schools all over Europe; universally, the best vocational schools are those operated by the Dutch.

For example, a Dutch vocational school training shipyard workers is propitiously located on the docks in Rotterdam, the world's largest port. A vocational school training chefs and bakers is located in an old castle in Holland. Whenever possible the Dutch vocational school is located at, or in the heart of, the industry which its students are expected to serve.

By concentrating on training on the job, American schools can accomplish the same effective training, and perhaps even better. The important thing is to get the trainees out of the artificial atmosphere of the schools and into viable on-the-job training situations.

VOCATIONALESE

Evidence of the lack of insight which the vocational educators have into vocational training is seen in the perfectly dreadful pedagese which they have developed and use for describing the various vocational curricula. For example, the terms used to describe most programs are "vocational technical education," "vocational education," and "occupational education." Actually the term "occupational education" adequately describes the entire field as well as the pre-vocational training programs which are being developed in the junior high and elementary schools. This term should be used as the rubric under which all vocational programs are contained. It is all inclusive and more accurately describes this type of education than any of the other existing terms. Another illustration of the confusion in terminology is the program which deals with training students to be salesmen. This is called "diversified cooperative education"; the program which involves youngsters in a variety of merchandising and trade fields is named "distributive education."

CAREER MARKETEERS

Actually, the teachers in these programs are career marketeers. Their chief function is the marketing of occupations and career opportunities for high school students. Training of these individuals should, therefore, be in the field of marketing and business rather than education.

The training of guidance counselors shows a reckless disregard for high school students because the major emphasis in most teacher-training institutions is on how to deal with the college-bound; yet over 60% of high school graduates do not get any formal education after high school. As a result, high school students are either ill-advised or receive no career advice whatever, which results in inappropriate involvement on the part of many.

Since it has been estimated that by 1980 only 20% of the job opportunities will require a college degree, the fallacy of vocational education is seen in the statistics which report that only 14% of all high school students are enrolled in vocational educational programs.

What the schools need, in the place of co-operative type operations, are teams of marketing people whose purpose is to help young people enter appropriate occupations and then see that they are properly trained.

By moving from in-house vocational education programs to community co-op programs, the vocational department of a school will have clusters of occupations available for its students.

The purpose of the career marketeer is to:

1) Help high school students select an appropriate occupation.
2) Arrange for them to enter training in a community business by contracting with a local entrepreneur.
3) Measure their achievement from time to time.

4) Schedule payment to the contractor as the student reaches a certain occupational level.

Another important activity of a career marketeer is to arrange mini courses on a seminar type basis within the school on the various occupations which are available within the community. The purpose of a mini course on an occupation is to give students the information and background which they need in order to select an appropriate occupation.

PROGRAM COMPONENTS

The necessary happenings in a viable occupational education program serving youth effectively are as follows:

1. Occupational information coupled with job orientation.
2. A pre-vocational analysis of interest.
3. A pre-vocational analysis of aptitude in the field of interest.
4. A diagnosis of communication skills already acquired and a determination of additional needs.
5. A program of training in civic responsibility.
6. Performance contracted on the job training.
7. Checkpoint evaluation of performance.
8. Placement and checkpoint follow-up.

THE RESUMÉ

In the analysis and subsequent training in communication skills, it is important for the student to receive specific and appropriate training in the writing of the resumé. The technique for selling one's self is one of the basic skills in which every vocationally trained student should be proficient. What specifically should be covered here? The resumé is a short, condensed, but very much to-the-point history of an individual's education, activities, accomplishments, and employment. The concentration of any resumé should revolve around the individual's growth, in order that the prospective employer can have a clear perspective of his prospect for success and advancement. The student should be prepared to defend or expand on any element in the resumé at an appropriate discussion during the subsequent interview.

THE TRUSTEE CONCEPT

One of the reasons that vocational education has been so poor is the lack of serious involvement on the part of businessmen and labor leaders. Actually federal guidelines for vocational education demand their participation by requiring that each program have an advisory committee. This approach is a travesty. What happens is that the vocational education teacher in a program sets up a committee which seldom meets and has little insight into what is going on.

If vocational education is to be as strong a part of the curriculum as it needs to be, then businessmen and labor leaders must be much more involved. It is recommended that each local school system set up an autonomous group of businessmen to develop policies and guidelines for occupational education within a community. This supervisory detachment should have the power and prestige of a college board of trustees. This grouping of business and labor leaders should have broad policy-making power in order to give the proper leadership to occupational education programs.

A BALANCED PROGRAM

In the comprehensive high school curriculum of the seventies, high school students who have a need for or an interest in occupational training should have access to programs which provide a balance between academic work and occupational training. This concept allows any student beyond the ninth grade to select a course of study which will not require more than three hours a day in the formal atmosphere of the school. The rest of his school program can take place in on-the-job training in a business or trade which suits his interest, motivation and qualifications.

The programs at the school should contain sufficient flexibility to enable the student to obtain the formal three hours of schooling which he needs either in the morning, afternoon, or evening.

The formal part of a student's program should be largely elective, with only three subjects required beyond the ninth grade. The required curricula should be in the area of the language arts, mathematics and biology. All other subjects should be elective.

SUMMARY

What is wrong with existing vocational education programs?

1. Students are not adequately trained for job entry.
2. Schools are constructing expensive shops which duplicate facilities available in the community.
3. Educators trained academically who are in decision-making positions about vocational education are often unconcerned about occupational training.
4. Educators have failed to recognize the schools' responsibility for individuals who are not in school but who need occupational training.
5. Vocational counseling is incompetent.

What is burgeoning to solve these problems? A new awareness of the importance of occupational education is taking place everywhere among educators. Educators have begun to recognize that if the schools are to continue to receive public support, then they must be geared to accommodate all of the learning needs in the community.

The concept of performance contracting offers great promise of becoming the unifying force between the school and the community as the schools become proficient at contracting vocational programs with community businesses. This makes the community an extension of the school and opens many new avenues for education and training.

8

The Rights and Privileges of Students in the Comprehensive High School

While most people, and all school administrators, deplore activism among students, no one has written a treatise which properly pinpoints the legal basis for student dissent. The right of students to protest against school rules, regulations, and authority was established by no less an institution than the United States Supreme Court. So many of today's societal problems were laid at the door of the U.S. Supreme Court during the era of Chief Justice Warren that I am reluctant to add another, but in the interest of authentic historicity, there is no other choice.

Dissent on the part of college youth dates back no earlier than 1965. The promulgating factors were the twin issues of Civil Rights and the Vietnam War. Dissent at the high school level has an even shorter history, beginning in 1967, but it was generated by entirely different factors. While a considerable amount of high school disruption has resulted from school desegregation, most of it has been caused by stifling administrative rules, an inappropriate curriculum, and mediocre teaching methods.

THE HISTORY OF DISSENT

Historically the first great dissenter over a civil rights issue was Henry David Thoreau. Rugged individualist that he was, Thoreau went to jail rather than pay his poll tax. When Ralph Waldo

Emerson visited Thoreau in jail, he was surprised by the question, "Why aren't you here too, Waldo?"

Youthful activists in both high schools and colleges have adopted the Thoreau strategy and many underground newspapers use Thoreau's famous different drummer statement on either the front page or the masthead of their paper.

> If a man does not keep pace with his companions, perhaps it is because he hears a different drummer. Let him step to the music which he hears, however measured or far away.

STUDENTS AND THE COURTS

Recent decisions of the United States Supreme Court have greatly eroded the authority with which schools have customarily dealt with their students. The Courts have clearly established that the basic freedoms of life, liberty, and the pursuit of happiness are given to all Americans by the Bill of Rights and strengthened by the Fourteenth Amendment.

Since the beginning, we have thought that these freedoms applied only to adults 21 years of age, or over, but the Supreme Court has recently determined that students have these freedoms and can exercise them when in school.

The students' new freedoms have their origin in two famous Supreme Court cases. The first legal breakthrough in students' rights happened when the High Court ruled on whether students could be compelled to pledge allegiance to the flag. In making its decision the Court went far beyond the issue of the flag, and ruled as follows in the case of West Virginia vs. Barnette, Supra:

> The Fourteenth Amendment, as now applied to the States, protects the citizen against the State itself and all of its creatures—Boards of Education not excepted. These have, of course, important, delicate, and highly discretionary functions, but none that they may not perform within the limits of the Bill of Rights. That they are educating the young for citizenship is reason for scrupulous protection of Constitutional freedoms of the individual, if we are not to strangle the free mind at its source and teach youth to dis-

count important principles of our government as mere platitudes.

When the Court went so far as to determine that students in
school should be protected against boards of education, it opened
Pandora's box. School board members are traditionally local citizens who are interested in better schools and better communities.
Except in Florida and one or two other states they serve without
remuneration.

The Barnette decision did much more than merely extend student rights. It greatly weakened the concept of local control and
local support of schools. Most school board members are highly
incensed over a High Court decision which states that students need
protection from them.

When the Barnette case, which set forth the legal basis for
dissent, was adjudicated in October of 1942, there was a war going on and the times were not favorable to student protest. It was
the Tinker decision in 1968 which reaffirmed student freedom as
outlined in the Barnette case that really got things going.

THE TINKER CASE

The second important decision affecting student rights was the
now famous Tinker case.[12] In this adjudication, the Tinker children and their friends insisted on wearing black arm bands to
school to protest the Vietnam War. After the school principal suspended them from school, their parents sued in the courts and
won not only the right to wear arm bands, but complete freedom
of speech and action "in school as well as out of school" for all
students.

When Mr. Justice Fortas delivered the opinion of the Court in
the Tinker Case, all would have been well had he merely ruled that
the children had the right to wear arm bands. Instead, he went on
to interpret the First Amendment as giving children equal rights
with adults. This had the effect of destroying the concept of *in loco*

---

[12] The Supreme Court Decision in the case of John F. Tinker and Mary Beth
Tinker, Minors, etc., et al., Petitioners, v. Des Moines Independent Community
School District et al. has such great significance that it is reprinted in its entirety
in the Appendix since reprints are not available from either the Clerk of the
Supreme Court or the Government Printing Office.

parentis which has been the basis for school discipline from time immemorial. Justice Stewart, who concurred in the decision to permit the wearing of arm bands, wrote in his concurrence: "I cannot share the Court's uncritical assumption that, school discipline aside, the First Amendment rights of children are coextensive with those of adults."

JUSTICE BLACK'S DISSENT

The dissent of Mr. Justice Black was far more vigorous. He pointed out, succinctly, that the Court had eroded the authority of the schools to discipline its students:

> The Court's holding in this case ushers in, what I deem to be an entirely new era, in which the power to control pupils by the elected officials of state supported public schools in the United States, is in ultimate effect transferred to the Supreme Court. . . .

> The Court brought this particular case here on a petition for certiorari urging that the First and Fourteenth Amendments protect the right of school pupils to express their political views all the way "from kindergarten through high school". . . .

> One defying pupil was Paul Tinker, eight years old, who was in the second grade; another, Hope Tinker, was eleven years old in the fifth grade; a third member of the Tinker family was thirteen in the eighth grade; a fourth member of the same family was John Tinker, fifteen years, and an eleventh grade high school pupil. . . . And I repeat that if the time has come when pupils of state-supported schools, kindergarten, grammar school or high school, can defy, flaunt orders of school officials to keep their minds on their own school's work, it is the beginning of a new revolutionary era of permissiveness in this country fostered by the judiciary. The next logical step, it appears to me, would be to hold unconstitutional laws that bar pupils under 21 or 18 from voting, or from being elected members of the Boards of Education. . . .

> The original idea of schools, which I do not believe is yet abandoned as worthless or out of date, was that children

had not reached the point of experience and wisdom which enabled them to teach all of their elders. It may be that the Nation has outworn the old-fashioned slogan that "children are to be seen, not heard," but one may, I hope, be permitted to harbor the thought that taxpayers send children to school on the premise that at their age they need to learn, not teach. . . .

While, as Justice Black pointed out, it now appears that the courts may have gone too far in taking away the authority of duly appointed school personnel, it should be kept in mind that the schools have, in the past, grossly abused their authority.

The interesting thing about recent court decisions is that they have switched from support of the schools to support of the students. Up until the Barnette decision, the courts nearly always reinforced the authority of the schools. For example, in 1923 an 18-year-old girl was expelled from school by a school board in Arkansas which had adopted a regulation forbidding students to use cosmetics. The court upheld the school board's right to take this action. However, since 1942, when the Barnette decision was handed down, the courts have been more inclined to question the authority of the school and support the defending student who was in violation of school regulations.

THE REASONABLE EXERCISE OF AUTHORITY

The dilemma of the principal in the welter of unfavorable court decisions is a serious one. The courts have tossed him from pillar to post and even his own professional organization which he considers his most supportive ally has been unable to help.

The National Association of Secondary School Principals was organized for the specific purpose of strengthening the high school principalship. In a major effort to assist the principal find his way through the maze of court cases favoring students' rights, the National Association of Secondary School Principals published in 1969 a booklet, *Reasonable Exercise of Authority,* highlighting the various cases involving both state and federal jurisdictions. Cases highlighted dealt with behavior codes, appearances, freedom of expression, right of petition, and other sensitive areas.

What this well-intentioned publication may have accomplished was to confuse the issue of administrative authority even further. It established the point that court decisions have been so contradictory that no clear delineation of authority can be laid down at this point in history.

The commanding reason for probing the area of court decisions and attempting to provide the principal with guidelines as expressed by the attorneys heading this effort is given as "in the hope such information will help them stay out of the courts." Unfortunately, there is no way for principals to avoid getting into the courts. For example, principle number 3 in this publication states:

> 3. No student may pass out buttons or other literature during regular hours either in class or in the halls between classes.

Since this interpretation, principals have been legally enjoined by a number of courts for preventing the passing of both buttons and literature.

This publication's guidelines for establishing eligibility rules for elections to the student council are also being disregarded by the courts. The document recommends that eligibility rules for election to the Student Council be published and enforced. Yet the courts are now ruling that there should be no eligibility rules for candidacy to the office of student government representatives. Any student in the school should be eligible for this office. If democracy is to be served, say the courts, every student is worthy of being chosen, just as in the community any citizen is eligible to run for the city council. For far too long, according to some court decisions, the schools have required a grade average or some other ridiculous, illegal qualification as a prerequisite to filing for election. Full and free participation in student government should be encouraged with a thorough understanding by students that their action on the council will not affect college admission or job recommendation if it is in conflict with faculty or administration opinion.

Perhaps the greatest problem which this publication attempts to clear up is the matter of whether the principal has the right to search a student's desk or locker. The document handles this issue as follows:

> Many legal specialists, it is true, are of the opinion that the strictures in the Fourth Amendment against search and seizure probably are not applicable to a student's person or to his desk or locker. Nonetheless, we caution principals against any such searching except under extreme circumstances, unless permission to do so has been freely given by the student, the student is present, and other competent witnesses are at hand.

> Where drugs or weapons are suspected, the police should be contacted and the search conducted in keeping with accepted police procedures and with the principal or a designated faculty member present.

The courts are now delineating between the search of a student's person and his desk or locker. Recent decisions indicate that the Constitution protects a student's person but does not prohibit a search of public property such as desks or lockers.

The most significant conclusion of the *Reasonable Exercise of Authority* is the fact that students who create serious or chronic discipline problems are entitled to due process before disciplinary action may be taken. This means, in effect, that if the school administrator decides to suspend a student for misconduct he must:

1. Provide notice in writing of the charges.
2. Draft a summary of evidence on which the charges are based.
3. Allow the right of a formal hearing with the student's parents or attorney.
4. Give the student the right of cross-examination.

School principals simply do not have time for this sort of activity and if the schools are ever to get on with the business of teaching and learning, then this must be clearly understood. Students in school should not be entitled to due process when they have flagrantly violated school rules.

The deplorable thing about the NASSP publication is that in its precedent-setting demand for due process and on a variety of other issues it goes far beyond the decision of the courts in limiting the authority of the school principal. On the contrary, the organization should be demanding legislation which will support the position of the principal in his effort to maintain law, order, and a reasonable climate for learning.

GUIDELINES FROM THE U.S. COMMISSIONER

Traditionally, the role of the U.S. Commissioner of Education has been to administer federal programs. There is no precedent for the Commissioner's involvement or concern for the internal administrative affairs of high schools.

Yet student disorder, generated by the new freedom given by the Tinker Decision, had reached such a crescendo by the summer of 1969 that former Commissioner James E. Allen, Jr., wrote two letters, giving advice and suggesting guidelines for the schools to operate under during the school year 1969–70. His concern was to abate some of the disorder in the schools.

One of these letters was directed to the Chief State School Officers of the various states and the other to the secondary school principals. This is probably the first time a Commissioner has ever bothered to write letters about the internal operations of the schools.

Because of the precedence and significance of this event both of the Commissioner's letters setting forth guidelines for handling student unrest are reprinted here. The advice which they contain is sage, pertinent, and timely.

DEPARTMENT OF HEALTH, EDUCATION,
AND WELFARE
OFFICE OF EDUCATION
WASHINGTON, D.C. 20202

SPECIAL MESSAGE TO CHIEF STATE
SCHOOL OFFICERS ON STUDENT UNREST

FROM

JAMES E. ALLEN, JR.
ASSISTANT SECRETARY FOR EDUCATION
AND
U.S. COMMISSIONER OF EDUCATION

I have become increasingly concerned about student unrest at the secondary school level. During a four-month period in the past school year, over 340 secondary schools in 38 states experienced serious student disturbances. The number of incidents is likely to increase this year as junior and senior high school students join in the general activism which has become so characteristic of our times.

Educational leaders have an obligation to confront the issues which underlie unrest and to plan actions which reduce avoidable tensions in our school districts. All of us need to be thinking through what we can do about the problem. A few days ago, I sent you an advance copy of a Message to Secondary School Principals which I prepared at the invitation of the National Association of Secondary School Principals. It raised some basic questions and encouraged principals to take the initiative in finding answers for their schools in conjunction with boards of education, parents, teachers and students.

I should now like to share with you some initial ideas about specific steps which communities may find constructive in dealing with some of the underlying causes of student unrest. I hope these ideas will begin an exchange of ideas between us on this complicated issue. This list may be helpful to you at this time for your planning to assist school districts in your State. I believe steps such as these would have a positive effect on reducing some of the more common causes of tension in secondary schools today.

Short Range Steps:

1. The establishment of channels for open communication with and among students, teachers, paraprofessionals, parents and community leaders through greater personal accessibility, special study groups, advisory committees, informal luncheon dialogues and more involvement in community affairs and community problems by school personnel, including students.

2. The establishment of structures within the school which allow for the involvement of students in substantive educational planning through specific projects and task forces which deal not only with existing offerings but

explore new ideas such as field work in the community, independent study, short term seminars, etc.

3. If dress codes are believed necessary, they should be established with student and parent participation, and should respect a student's self-image, allow for differences and promote intergroup respect rather than conformity to a single value system with its implied superiority. Students with different backgrounds and life styles need to feel accepted in their school if they are to respect it and have a feeling of belonging to that school.

4. The introduction of Black, Brown and other ethnic studies into existing courses and through additional offerings—developed collaboratively by students, teachers and administrators—to increase understanding, rather than fear, of cultural differences.

5. The review of policies for selecting students for honors and special recognition, such as cheerleading squads and prom queens, to assure such policies are equitable and unifying of school spirit rather than divisive.

6. The review of suspension and other disciplinary rules and the greater involvement of students in the maintenance of school discipline through student committees, student monitoring and honor systems. Provision of appeals or review procedures on disciplinary actions as a means to increase confidence both in school and in the community. Consideration might be given to involving students in development of a "Bill of Rights and Responsibilities" for the school.

7. The concerted effort to increase participation in extracurricular activities through more varied offerings, creative recruiting, convenient scheduling and special transportation so that every student will actively participate in at least one activity which is meaningful to him.

8. The establishment of committees to include school board members, administrators, students, teachers, paraprofessionals, parents, community organizations, and police to set up guidelines which insure the safety, protection and

rights of all persons in the school community and spell out carefully how and under what conditions law enforcement agencies will be used during disorders.

9. The establishment of orderly and well publicized procedures for the registering of legitimate grievances by parents and students so that there are alternatives to demonstrations and disorder. Possible initiation of an ombudsman or community liaison role to facilitate communication.

10. The broader utilization of individual teachers, to whom students respond readily, in areas of responsibility outside of the classroom.

Long Range Steps:

1. The provision of intensive in-service training for all school personnel—professional and nonprofessional—to encourage attitudes of respect for the dignity of all individuals and to value rather than reject diverse cultural backgrounds. While additional funds would be desirable for such programs, priority could be given with current in-service funds to this kind of training or by using existing community resources with little additional cost.

2. The expansion of training for teachers and supervisors in new methods of educating poor, minority group students and potential dropouts, placing special emphasis on early childhood education.

3. The careful reexamination and reorganization of grouping or tracking systems which may promote racial and socioeconomic segregation within a comprehensive desegregated school.

4. Introduction of stepped-up recruiting programs to obtain and promote many more minority group professionals and nonprofessionals in all schools at all levels of responsibility and authority.

5. The elimination of inequities in the instructional resources of schools within any school district (class sizes, age and relevance of textbooks, library resources, spe-

cial facilities, etc.) and the involvement of students in developing new instructional offerings for the future.

6. The employment of more community aides not only to assist with operations of the school and classroom but to assist school personnel in understanding the community and its families and how to utilize fully the learning opportunities outside of school.

7. The encouragement of decentralization of administration and authority to promote greater community involvement and identity with schools. Greater use of schools as community centers for educational and recreational purposes within the community.

8. The upgrading of vocational-technical offerings and counselling for students who do not plan to continue their formal schooling beyond high school graduation, so that they feel their opportunities are of at least the same quality as the college preparatory programs and so that they find greater relevancy in learning through service and work experiences in the community, closer ties to local business and industry, and familiarization with post high school opportunities in community colleges which may be nearby.

There is nothing startlingly new in these suggestions nor are they all inclusive by any means. You will have more to suggest I am sure. I offer them at this time only with the hope that they will assist your current efforts to alert the school districts of your State to the need for responsive educational planning and change in an era of growing student unrest. We can bemoan current conditions or we can seize upon them to improve the educational opportunities for all of our young people. I prefer the second course and urge you to join me in this effort.

We are giving the issue of student unrest high priority in our thinking and planning at the Office of Education for the coming months. I would welcome your reactions to these initial ideas and hope you will keep me informed of successful practices and actions in your State which may be useful to others. It is my intent to follow up these initial messages with subsequent reports to you on student unrest. I also encourage you to send me any suggestions of how the Office of Education can be of service to you in meeting this critically important challenge to the future of our schools.

Sincerely,
James E. Allen, Jr.

September 2, 1969

DEPARTMENT OF HEALTH,
EDUCATION, AND WELFARE
OFFICE OF EDUCATION
WASHINGTON, D.C. 20202

A MESSAGE TO THE NATION'S
SECONDARY SCHOOL PRINCIPALS

FROM

JAMES E. ALLEN, JR.
ASSISTANT SECRETARY FOR EDUCATION
AND
U.S. COMMISSIONER OF EDUCATION

The 1960's have been an era of unrest in our Nation's schools. The secondary school principal is increasingly in the center of conflicting pressures resulting from what seems to be a growing militancy. That more and more school administrators across the country have found ways to be responsive to these pressures in a productive manner is a credit to all concerned and to the education profession.

As the 1969–70 school year begins, I want to share with you some thoughts about one of the pressures confronting you and am grateful to the National Association of Secondary School Principals for making this possible. The unrest of students in our secondary schools has attracted less attention to date in the mass media than disturbances on college campuses. Many feel, however, that such student unrest will increase. The potential is there. Just in terms of numbers there are approximately 26,000 public secondary schools in the country compared to 1,600 four-year public and private colleges and universities and these secondary schools enroll 3 times as many students of a younger, more volatile age.

Thoughtful school administrators across the land in communities of all sizes and makeup are considering how best to cope with possible student disorders. This certainly is appropriate and needs to be carefully thought out in advance of such incidents. But it is even more important that we address ourselves forthrightly to the issues which underlie student unrest.

Our students are telling us that change is needed in our schools. Indeed, much of what they call for has been urged by many principals and other educators in the past. Concerns and reforms presented by our students are important and warrant careful consideration. Perhaps by responding to them patiently and thoughtfully, we can help make the 1970's an era of productive change in our Nation's schools.

I urge you to take the initiative in bringing together, as this new school year begins, groups representative of all segments interested in your school to identify key issues of concern and to determine what alternatives there are for achieving appropriate changes in the policies and practices of your school. While each community will have its own agenda of issues, let me suggest some which seem to be arising in schools across the country:

1. How can we assure that public schools indeed are *public* in the sense that citizens whose children are served feel their schools are responsive and responsible to them?

2. How can we make the educational offerings of our schools more relevant to the society from which our students come and to the world of work for which our students are preparing?

3. How can we further improve and objectively measure the quality of teaching in our schools to the end that

public confidence in the performance of our schools will be enhanced?

4. How can our schools be more effectively managed through greater and more meaningful sharing of decision-making responsibility and authority with parents, teachers and students?

5. How can we encourage good citizenship in the future by assuring broader rights and responsibilities of citizenship for students in the rules and regulations of our schools?

6. How can we tangibly demonstrate greater cultural awareness and respect for the racial and ethnic groups represented in our schools?

7. How can we establish orderly channels for the registering of legitimate concerns by those our schools serve so that there are alternatives to confrontation and demonstration?

These are not easy questions nor are they all inclusive. But they are basic to education in a democratic society. No one person can adequately answer them. But boards of education, administrators, teachers, parents and students can seek answers for their own schools that will be more meaningful than any "outside" answers.

Seeking greater communication in a vacuum is impossible. Searching for it in the midst of turmoil is at best difficult. I urge you to take the initiative in seeking communication with your constituents on issues which affect your school as a means of opening new opportunities for support of educational change. This role of educational leader—indeed statesman—is one for which the secondary school principals of our Nation are admirably suited by their training, responsibilities and experience.

Let us all do our utmost to make 1969–70 a landmark year —a year of communication, responsiveness and relevant change. I assure you I shall do everything I can to join with you in this effort.

August 29, 1969

THE DISREGARD OF ADVICE

It is indeed unfortunate that Commissioner Allen's letters were largely ignored. They should have been taken as gospel and used as basic guidelines. If this had happened, a great deal of school disruption could have been prevented.

Certainly, the issue of representation by blacks on cheerleading teams, which is one of the issues on which he gave directions, was one of the major factors causing disruption in the school years 1969–70, 1970–71, and 1971–72.

Regrettably, his letters were ignored and student disorder was rampant. Perhaps the grossest example of what the Commissioner was talking about and one that could have been prevented by his guidelines was the disruption of the Rockledge High School in Rockledge, Florida, where a black cheerleader who did not maintain a certain grade average was suspended. The outcome was a year of school upheaval, followed by a complete change in the administrative and coaching staff. Had the advice of the Commissioner's guidelines been followed, the incident would never have occurred, but the schools disregarded his letters and the Rockledge case has been multiplied throughout the land during the past two school years.

THE FOOTBALL ISSUE

In his recommendations for short-range steps designed to eliminate divisiveness in the schools, Commissioner Allen strongly recommended a review of policies for the election of cheerleaders. These policies generally require a grade average of C. While some few schools have eliminated requirements for cheerleaders, all schools are still requiring rigid rules for participating in football.

Football, like cheerleading and the student council, should be open to participation by all students, whether they have passing grades or not. It should be the student's inalienable right to participate in extra class activities as long as he is in good standing behavior-wise as a student.

Unfortunately the grade average requirement for football players is set by state athletic associations. Since these are controlled by coaches and principals, it will probably require court action to strike them down.

DESEGREGATION AS AN ISSUE

The racial issues causing trouble in high schools other than the black cheerleader issue, are usually centered around demands for courses in black history and literature. Many schools have made a conscientious effort to offer these courses but the problem is a difficult one. Prior to 1900 there were no novels written by blacks except on the subject of slavery. There were no important dramas written by blacks prior to 1920.

What the schools should do is not simply put in crash programs of black studies, but carefully re-examine their entire curriculum offerings. For example, practically every high school in the country requires English literature for all of its students. The reason, of course, is because of the Anglo Saxon heritage of the majority of American people. Yet the blacks with their African ancestry couldn't care less about British literature. Nor is it fair to require them to study it. So, what is really needed is a careful and in-depth re-analysis of the entire program of studies.

THE STUDENTS FOR DEMOCRATIC SOCIETY ISSUE

The SDS is an organization preaching anarchy both in the schools and in society which should be outlawed whenever it makes an appearance.

The major impact of the SDS on disruption in the high school is the publication of the booklet *High School Reform* written by a California high school activist. This paper, advocating high school reform, was circulated in mimeographed form for a couple of years, and published for wider distribution by the Students for a Democratic Society in 1967.

The purpose of the position paper was to inform high school students on the best techniques for "taking over a high school." Strategies for accomplishing this task were described as follows:

1. Demonstrate contempt for student government.
2. Contact the local ACLU attorney and ascertain the full extent of students' rights.

3. Start an underground newspaper.
4. Seek support from the Unitarian Church and the American Federation of Teachers.

Supposedly the Unitarian Church was singled out because of its intellectual and liberal approach to issues. The AFT undoubtedly was used as a result of a strong position statement which it adopted on students' rights.

The SDS is presently in a state of decline and the schools should vigorously oppose any revival of high school chapters affiliated with this organization.

THE COMMUNICATION PROBLEM

When one examines the myriad reports of schools which have been disrupted by student activism the one characteristic which stands out is the lack of communication which has existed between the administration of the school and the students who have taken leading roles in the activism. In most cases there has been a complete failure to communicate. The absence of communication in events leading to disruption is comparable to communication between Maine and Texas at the time the first telegraph line connecting them was constructed. When Henry David Thoreau heard that a telegraph was being built which would link Maine to Texas he commented:

> "We are in a great haste to construct a magnetic telegraph from Maine to Texas, but Maine and Texas it may be will have nothing important to communicate to each other."

This is the same situation which has existed between students and the administrators of high schools. They have simply had "nothing important to communicate to each other."

SUMMARY

When one examines carefully the high school complex and its operation there are some obviously disturbing trends which must be reversed. Epitomized, these are as follows:

1. The growing bureaucracy which separates the administration from its students thus widening an already critical gap.
2. The isolation of the school and its programs from learning opportunities in the community.
3. The lack of alternatives to the high school academic program.
4. Girls are being openly discriminated against by requiring them to take courses in home economics and by not providing them with vocational programs comparable to those offered boy students.

Because of these factors the schools are reflecting less and less the interests of the community and larger society which it is organized to serve.

One of the functions of the school which has had scant or no attention is a serious effort on the part of the school and its staff for students to enjoy learning. The student should be expected to enjoy high school and look forward to further learning, either on the job or on entry into college. The schools must come to recognize that everyone should develop an interest in continuing learning after leaving the environs of high school.

RECOMMENDATIONS

The erosion of authority is resulting in a simultaneous lowering of standards, all under the banner of "freedom" and self-expression. The result is a general blurring of standards so that it is not really clear what the school's purpose and goals are or how it is to achieve them.

The most needed thing in American education today is a clarification and restatement of national goals, especially educational goals. These should be established by a Presidential Commission. Some attempt at restructuring national goals was made during President Eisenhower's time. He appointed a Commission on National Goals and the Commission's report on goals for education was of some help to the schools but unfortunately, the Commission expired before the job was finished.

The Tinker case and its subsequent erosion of the school's authority has created such a debacle in the schools that there is now a serious crisis in confidence in the public schools. This crisis can be resolved only if it is attacked at all levels. There is an urgent need for leadership to begin in the White House with the appointment of a Presidential Commission to establish new national goals in education. The purpose of this Commission should be to clearly establish the goals which the public schools are expected to reach. It should also recommend new legislation to fill the void in authority which was created by the Supreme Court. School teachers and administrators must have some clear cut authority if they are to house, manage, and direct learning for several thousand young but immature citizens all under one roof.

9

Pros and Cons
of the Year-Round School

A PHANTASMAGORICAL CARROT

When the role of the high school changes from that of a limited institution, serving teenagers an academic fare, to a broadly comprehensive institution, it becomes an operating base for a wide variety of educational action. In this type of institution a high school subject becomes, in the words of Eugene Youngert, "Anything which a student can study with profit and pleasure."

As a part of the reformation of the traditional institution into a broad flexible institution, every possible innovative expediency must be examined. Since many educators are urging Year-Round Schooling as a panacea, this concept and its appropriateness is analyzed in this chapter.

After a careful study of the kind of program which year-round advocates are promoting, and participating in their national seminar on the Year-Round School, the author is convinced that the issue is not a viable one. The summer months and their time for relaxation without formal education are important to the individual and his non-school learnings. Every modern high school graduate should have the benefit of work experiences, service experiences, and travel experiences before leaving high school. These happenings are best accomplished in the summer for a variety of reasons.

---

[13] This chapter is based on unpublished research conducted by William P. Shaw of the Charles F. Kettering Foundation of Dayton, Ohio.

But, a total evaluation of Year-Round Schooling and its implications is highly appropriate to the comprehensive high school and the new developments which are influencing it.

The dictionary describes the word "phantasmagoria" as a shifting series of illusions or deceptions. The Year-Round School is that kind of mirage. Voltaire once said, "There is nothing so important as an idea whose time has come." Paraphrased, this great sage's comment would be: "There is nothing quite so unimportant as an idea whose time has passed." This is what has happened to the notion of twelve-month schooling. It is an idea whose time has come and gone, and come and gone again.

Educators all over the country are meeting to discuss promoting the year-round school and "making the idea come again." This should not be a difficult task. Historically, year-round schooling was a hot idea in 1904. In that year many education articles glowingly described "a school year of twelve months." Subsequent revivals of the year-round schooling notion occurred in 1924, 1947, and 1963.

The twelve-month school year has been resurrected so often that it calls to mind the mythological Phoenix. This fabled bird was able to burn itself to ashes and rise again later, more a paragon than before. So it is with the twelve-month school year. This old chestnut has been abandoned time and again as impractical, unnecessary, and unwanted, but it always arises a decade or so later as a bright new heresy. Since no school system has ever been able to operate a year-round school successfully, or even justify the viability of the concept for once and for all time, this "old wine in new bottles" routine should be put back in its old familiar archives and allowed to rest in eternal peace.

THE HISTORY OF THE MOVEMENT

For the sake of historicity, it is important to examine the history of the year-round school movement. In 1900, Bluffton, Indiana, was the first system to try a year-round program. Newark, New Jersey, instituted it in 1912; Amarillo, Texas, in 1920; and Aliquippa, Pennsylvania, in 1928. After from ten to twenty years of experimentation with year-round schooling, each of these cities abandoned the idea because of four unsolvable problems: (1) complexities of scheduling, (2) confusion of four different enrollments, (3) chaos in promotions and graduation, and (4) a multitude of other problems.

NEWARK'S EXPERIENCE

With reference to Newark's experience, an excerpt from a letter from Mr. Franklin Titus, the Superintendent of Schools, is of interest. Mr. Titus writes as follows:

> The Newark public schools had an all-year program during the period from 1912–1931. The program was terminated by the Newark Board of Education in 1931, primarily because the all-year schools ceased to be sufficiently appropriate, adaptable, and serviceable to the needs of the community and the public. The program was inaugurated in 1912, largely as an attempt to render special assistance to the children and parents with foreign backgrounds residing in overcrowded and underprivileged neighborhoods. It was hoped that additional school time spent during the summer would serve as a remedial instrument to improve or accelerate such children, especially in the special subjects area.

Why was the Newark program abolished after 19 years? In the words of the superintendent, the program was aborted because:

> Ultimately, the related criticism was advanced, that these pupils were not only still ill-prepared languagewise and academically, but from the viewpoint of chronological age and social maturity they were not ready to adjust to the chronological and social ages of the rest of the secondary schools' pupil population. Finally, the plan was abandoned in 1931, in view of the widespread lack of satisfaction which evidenced itself throughout the community.

Bluffton, Amarillo, Aliquippa, Newark—these are but a few of the "booms and busts" in year-round schooling. Epitomized, this activity has had more opportunities to prove itself than a little boy has chances in a candy shop.

FROM THEORY TO PRACTICE

Unquestionably the leading theoretician of the year-round school year is Professor George B. Glinke, Administrative Assistant for Year-Round Schools of the Utica, Michigan, School System. In a report to the Utica, Michigan, School System, Dr. Glinke recently said:

> One item which becomes very clear to this researcher, as involved with the year-round educational movement, is that the concept has moved from the theoretical stage on the college campus to the local public school district for eventual implementation. This has to be the breakthrough the movement has been waiting for.

First, it should be clearly established that this is not the way things happen in education. The innovations which have been successful have all originated in the schools, not on the college campuses. Nongradedness, team teaching in the elementary school, independent study, these are all school-developed improvements. The only previous innovation which originated on college campuses as theory is the concept of modular scheduling, and this proved to be a disaster causing great trouble to the schools which experimented with it.

The greatest perpetrators of the Year-Round Education movement are a group of educators who have banded together to push this concept. This group annually puts on a seminar on the topic of Year-Round Schools, and charges other educators a $75 fee to participate. It is amusing that most of this group, such as the Superintendent who hosted the 1971 Seminar, not only have no program of year-round schools in their own district, but they have no plans for implementing one. In other words, Year-Round Schools are fine for some other district.

THERE MAY ALREADY BE TOO MUCH SCHOOLING

Proponents of year-round schooling go at the notion as if time in school comprises the major part of a person's education.

This must be refuted. Sociologists have clearly established that people acquire their total knowledge from six major sources:

> the family
> peer groups
> personal experiences
> community organizations
> mass media
> and—the formal school.

Consider, please, that formal education is only one of the six spokes in the educational wheel; and if it is expanded, too much emphasis may be placed upon it. The importance of family, peers, mass media, and experiences of work and travel should not be overlooked in the educational game. Formal schooling has, in the past, occupied only 1/6 of an individual's total education background, and there is no evidence to support an increase of this activity at the expense of the others.

Actually, if educational research can be believed, students should be spending less time in school rather than more. James Coleman, in a major study for the U. S. Office of Education, concluded that only 15 percent of the time in school is learning time and is of any use to an individual. If this research is accepted as viable, and there is no reason to refute it, then we should be making a massive effort to improve what we are now doing rather than simply "adding more of the same."

COSTS

One of the significant considerations of the year-round school concept is cost. School systems which have experimented with year-round schooling report such mixed figures on cost that it is difficult to assess this factor. Nashville, Tennessee, reported that first year costs of year-round schooling increased operating expenses by 21 percent and that cost per pupil for the summer quarter was 64 percent higher than in other quarters. Lexington, Kentucky, found that the financing of year-round schooling required a 20-percent increase in taxes. It is interesting to note that none of the experiments report any saving or less cost, yet most of the backers of the concept give this as their chief reason.

The erstwhile Commissioner for New York, James Allen, suggest that year-round programs save money when the schools begin to graduate students early, thus offering classrooms and studies for other students. What he fails to tell us is—what do we do with the students who graduate early? Most 15- and 16-year olds are not mature enough to handle the new morality which abounds on college campuses, much less the easy access to drugs which exists on most campuses. And, for those 15- and 16-year old graduates who don't attend college, there is neither a job market nor prospects of one.

The Florida State Department of Education concluded after a major study several years ago that year-round schooling and the rotating four-quarter plan would not result in overall savings. The Florida Department estimated an annual statewide savings of $3,822,400 on depreciation and new buildings to be constructed in the future, but it anticipated new expenditures which would more than offset the amount saved. These new expenditures include:

1. An increased number of registrations, promotions, graduations, and examinations which would require more staff members and at least double the administrative costs of the large schools.
2. The reduction in pupil-teacher ratio which would increase instructional costs.
3. The decreased density of pupils transported on established bus routes which would lead to increased per-pupil transportation costs.
4. The installation of air conditioning which would result in increased additional capital outlay and operating costs.

In addition to the Florida State Department studies, the Florida Educational Research and Development Council in 1966 conducted a feasibility study of *seven* rescheduled school year plans for Polk County, Florida. The council concluded that the rotating four-quarter plan would result in a 25.21 percent increase in net expenditures.

From the aforementioned Florida studies it can be concluded that building costs would decrease about 16 percent over a long period of time due to a decrease in enrollment. It can be further speculated that building costs are offset by other costs which may run as high as 25 percent. For example:

1. Staggered plans tend to increase rather than decrease expenditures.
2. The only feasible all-year plans developed for reducing costs involve acceleration of pupils to reduce enrollment.
3. Financial savings do not occur. During the transition period, when a new pupil attendance flow pattern is taking over to eliminate one year of schooling, costs will be higher. These adjustment costs will be primarily for increased teacher salaries, retirement benefits, and matters of this kind.

The evidence is clear that year-round education increases the cost of schooling between 20 and 25 percent. This forces me to raise the specter of where the money is going to come from for year-round schools. There is a major taxpayers' rebellion extending throughout the length and breadth of the land, and school systems need to face up to the reality that they simply are not going to get any more money. According to a recent survey of the National Education Association, schools in 14 states are facing a crisis similar to the one in Ohio which has chosen several times in the last two years to close schools rather than fund them, and 18 other states are "feeling the effects of a severe financial pinch." Money may well be the decisive factor which torpedoes the present interest in an extended year.

It is unfortunate that the chief community backers of this movement are local chapters of the Junior Chambers of Commerce. The Jaycees are an enthusiastic and vocal group but rarely do they have the time to carefully analyze the projects which they sponsor so vigorously.

ORGANIZATION

From the standpoint of organization, most of the proposed plans include the use of the trimester, the split trimester, the quadrimester, or some variation of the multimester. Florida's experience with the trimester is pertinent here. The trimester was highly touted some six years ago when the Board of Regents, the state's board of higher education, with loud pronouncements of a great innovation adopted the trimester as a year-round program for the state's universities. Subsequently, some secondary schools like the famous Nova High School jumped on the band wagon and instituted a trimester program. The great accomplishments of the trimester were heralded in the *Nation's Schools* in April of 1964 in an article entitled "Trimester Plan Makes Nova Novel." Anyway, the whole notion of year-round schooling on the tri- mester plan was a disaster of considerable magnitude, and after several years of confusion, the Florida Board of Regents folded its tent like the Arabs and silently stole away—that is, it stole away from the trimester. Unfortunately, it is still cluttering up the rest of the educational scene with other nonsense.

The trimester in Florida's schools and colleges was a failure of monumental proportions. Despite this trauma, a group of educators advocating the year-round school in New York State is pushing for this desiccated approach to the year-round school. Their most recent effort is a booklet entitled "Setting the Stage for Lengthened School Year Programs," a special report designed for the governor of the State of New York. This booklet extols the virtue of the trimester as a significant new trend in school organization. It is inconceivable that New York educators have completely ignored the debacle created by the trimester in Florida. The ability of educators to overlook and disregard research is a unique talent peculiar to the field of professional education.

TEACHER OPINIONS

In considering year-round schooling, one must take into con- sideration the attitudes of teachers, parents, and students. Sur- veys of these groups indicate that they all may be in opposition. The big surprise is the resistance of teachers. It has generally been supposed that teachers would welcome the idea because they would receive more money, but this is not the case.

In a recent survey of teachers about year-round schools, the Lockport, Illinois, School System found that nearly 80 percent of the female teachers preferred the 180 day schedule. Of those polled, even the male teachers whose wives were employed, fa- vored the 180-day working year.

PARENT OPINIONS

In 1966, George Gallup conducted a national poll to determine how parents felt about year-round schooling. The Gallup Poll revealed that 76 percent of the parents were opposed to the four-quarter school plan. Sixty-eight percent of the parents opposed reducing the summer vacation period to four weeks and only four percent of the parents preferred year-round schooling when given the choice of twelve other alternatives.

Furthermore, one must consider the case of the family with several children in school under the quarter plan. There is no assurance that all the children would be free during the same quarter. In addition, if the father's vacation period is not flexible, the problem is more complicated. The gist of the matter is that there is no great support from parents for extending the school year.

STUDENT OPINIONS

What about the opinions of students? In an era in which there is so much democracy in the schools that it is difficult to tell who is holding the umbrella, it is imperative that student opinions be considered, and almost every high school today has set up various student advisory committees to advise on the curriculum and matters of instruction. While it is all right for educators to discuss educational matters, without involving students, away from home, it is imperative that student opinion have great weight when they go back to the ranch and start the "all-year" roundup.

In connection with student opinion, even very young children are alarmed about the specter of year-round schooling. A newspaper report of a ten-year-old girl's reaction to a proposal by the governor of South Carolina for the year-round program is of interest. The young lady's name is Evelyn Nolan. She is a fifth grader in Aiken, South Carolina. This is her letter:

Dear Governor West:

I read your statement and I refuse to go to 12 months of school. I will take three months of summer vacation, two

weeks of Christmas vacation, and New Year, and the day
before and the day after Thanksgiving and Friday, Saturday
and Sunday for Easter, and Friday and Monday for Valen-
tine, also.

Just think back when you were a boy. How would you
like going to school 12 months? How would you feel? Lousy,
or groovy?

It doesn't take much imagination to conjecture what position
most students will take about extended year schooling. One thing
is certain, and that is that their reaction will be both vociferous
and volatile. What has emerged with great clarity is the notion
that every student needs both a work experience and a service
experience before leaving high school. The schools have not been
providing these experiences and up to now, the only way students
could obtain them is during the summer when they are free to
obtain work experience on the job or service experience in hospitals, industry, social agencies, and businesses. The kind of educational opportunity available in these community institutions cannot and should not be duplicated in the school system. What the
schools should do is encourage participation in these learning activities both during the summer and during the regular school
year.

PRINCIPALS

Another group which must be considered when year-round
schools are proposed is the principals. When one considers operating a twelve-month school, the new student freedom and its
implications must be taken into consideration. There are literally
hundreds of schools across the country in which administrators
have been unable to control students on the nine- and ten-month
programs. Heaven help them if they take on the additional combat duty which is inherent in a year-round operation. The long
hot summers will be unbearable. It might be well to talk to some
principals who are veterans of combat duty before going too far
down the year-round school road. While this may sound like
caprice, there may be more truth than fiction here.

SPORTS

What about school athletics? No one has ever addressed himself properly to the question of what happens to school sports if students are not in school in the right quarter for certain sports. Nor is there any assurance that the various state athletic associations which control athletics and are composed of principals and coaches will allow deviation from the rules which polarize athletics.

QUESTIONS TO BE ANSWERED

One of the best sources of information about the year-round school is a publication by the Pennsylvania Department of Education titled "The Year-Round School." This publication is superb in the honesty with which it discusses both sides of the question. Most of the articles in journals are written by proponents of year-round schools, and they are all favorable. But with the Pennsylvania document there is a difference. The Pennsylvania publication cites, among other things, the ten most often asked questions about year-round activity.

1. Why did previous year-round programs fail?
2. Why does the length of the school year need changing? (a) To make the school more efficient, or (b) to effect economies.
3. What will the curriculum and program of instruction be for the year-round school?
4. Where will the school district obtain funds to cover initial costs of the year-round school?
5. What should school districts do with the additional time provided by a year-round program?
6. Will teachers, parents, and students want a year-round school?
7. How much will teachers be paid?
8. Will student acceleration be involved and, if so, how will acceleration be programmed?
9. What curriculum adjustments will be necessary for teachers if chronological age acceleration leads to the entrance

into secondary schools of entire classes that are a year or
so younger?

10. What adjustments will secondary school teachers have to
make if the elementary school keeps its children for a full
seven years but, in so doing, has them complete the equiv-
alent of the seventh grade curriculum before sending them
to junior high school?

THE VACATION PROBLEM

One of the great unanswered questions about year-round
schooling is the question of the traditional summer vacation. No
one has attempted to determine whether people will sociologically
alter their basic traditional vacation patterns to accommodate the
year-round schooling concept. It is very surprising that with a
complete absence of research on this topic, a group of educators
united for year-round schooling have assumed the stance of Ad-
miral Farragut at Mobile Bay: "Damn the torpedoes, full speed
ahead!"

True, there are a few advocates of winter sports who contend
that winter vacations are as good as, or superior to, summer vacations. But this group is a distinct minority. Winter, with its
time of colds and flu, so inhibits the activities of children that it
is absurd to think that the vacation cycle can be reversed.

Just as the year-round school is an idea whose time has passed,
there is a new movement burgeoning which appears to be an
idea whose time has come.

This is the movement in industry for a four-day week in order
that people can have three days of each week to devote to leisure
activities. Many people interpret the notion of a four-day week
as a further degeneration of the work ethic. The early settlers of
the country thought work was good and everybody should have
it, and the more of it a person had the better off he was. So.
people worked from dawn until dark. This ethic reached its most
perfect expression in the great hymn of yesterday, "Work, for the
Night Is Coming."

The work ethic, as a great American value, has now been bat-
tered to the point where it is highly vulnerable. The work week
has declined from 60 hours at the turn of the century to 40 hours

by 1940, and most of the labor strikes of the last year have included demands for a 25-hour week.

So, instead of pushing for an extended year, the schools should opt for a four-day school week for students and allow teachers one day for planning and developing the learning program. One of the reasons that classes are so dull and children learn so little is that over-burdened teachers do not have time for planning, consulting, and developing interesting and exciting learning activities. The idea of a four-day week is a new notion but one which deserves careful consideration.

In other words, instead of extending the time in school or even rearranging it on a year-round basis, the big need is for less time, better planning, and more quality in the things that are taught and learned. The only justification for extending the school year is to further effect the "keep the kids busy" syndrome.

Epitomized, in a world of turmoil over a four-day week for adults it is incongruous and completely anachronistic to espouse a five-day week and year-round schooling for the kids.

10

Conclusions
and Recommendations

Meeting the needs of secondary school students has been botched pretty badly all across the country. Everywhere, one finds well-funded, reasonably innovative high schools ridden by vandalism and hostility. Student resentment of what is taught and how the schools are managed is at a dangerously high pitch. In brief, the nation's high schools are in crisis. The first big question is why? The answer is found in the dichotomy between what the school says it does and what it actually does.

The avowed goal of most high schools is self-fulfillment for the individual. Take, as an example, the philosophy of Evanston Township High School of Evanston, Illinois. Every poll of outstanding schools taken during the past decade lists this school in the top five of the nation's high schools. The philosophy and objectives of this prestigious high school read as follows:

> Evanston Township High School seeks to provide a learning environment in which each student can develop self-identification, self-direction, and the skills and knowledge to use throughout life in his quest for self-fulfillment.[14]

And so it is all across the nation. All high schools have similar high-sounding phrases about the full expression of individuals in

---

[14] Annual Report of the Evanston Township High School, 1970–1971, p. 26.

their philosophies and objectives. But there, reality ends. The truth is that mass education and control of pupils, as the schools are presently organized, simply doesn't accommodate the quest of the individual for self-fulfillment. Yet, the schools insist that they are meeting these individual needs.

One of the major causes of clashes between students and the people who manage the schools centers around administrative control. While all administrations loudly proclaim individual development as their schools' objective, many of them jealously guard the right to hand out prestigious honors and recommendations based upon the subjective judgment of the administration, rather than some more democratic involvement. This is the principal factor in student disenchantment.

Heads of schools must cease such authoritarian acts as having the school's cheerleaders selected by faculty committees. Comprehensive extracurricular activities should be placed firmly in the hands of the student body. And individual curricular decisions must be put just as inflexibly under the dominion of the individual. Once this becomes a fait accompli, the schools will begin to turn the corner.

The greatest change needed in the high school must come from a new and serious look at the high school student. Today, a considerable number of high school students are eligible to vote. Those that are not eligible are approaching this new age of majority. Today's high school student is a new breed and must be dealt with in a new way.

The next great need is a change in the attitude of school principals. Instead of surrounding themselves with myriad administrative details, these individuals should be free to manage the learning process and they should have no other function.

How can a high school principal keep his head when all about him his fellow principals are losing theirs? As Charlie Keller, the great humanist, puts it, the high school administrator is "a 'fiddler on the roof,' trying to keep his balance, finding it difficult because something has happened to tradition." The problem is, can these fiddlers on the roof keep their balance, or are they, like Humpty Dumpty, in for a great fall? Many of them don't even seem to be aware that Rome is burning, but the fiddling goes on.

NEW CONCEPTS OF COMPREHENSIVENESS

Too many high schools are marking time, awaiting dramatic or revolutionary programs promised by various educational or business groups to transform them pumpkin-like into bright new heresies. It is now apparent that none of the national efforts is going to bring this about. If schools are to keep abreast of the changes in society and meet the needs of their students, the change must be initiated locally. Variations in the talents of teaching staffs, the abilities of students, community pressures and resources make every school an individual entity.

But there are guidelines which are appropriate to every school in varying degrees. Disenchantment with present programs is so great that every school should embark upon the kind of broadly comprehensive program which is expressed in the following components of the new comprehensive model:

Recommendation No. 1: General Education

Abolish the general education program which was so strongly recommended by James B. Conant in his recommendations for the Comprehensive High School in the fifties. In the seventies, the doctrine recently expressed by U.S. Commissioner of Education Sidney Marland is more appropriate: "The abomination known as general education should be abolished and replaced with contemporary career education in a comprehensive school."

Recommendation No. 2: The Restructured Day

The school day should be merged with the adult evening program to give a revised structure to the school day. The newly structured school day must offer courses all during the day and evening in order that students can have broader opportunities and more flexible time for work and service experiences at the time that these happenings are in operation in the community. This does not imply doubling or tripling the present school staff. It does infer redeployment.

For those schools that do not have adult education programs

which they can use as pivotal points in restructuring the school day, the school's library must serve as the pivot. The library must remain open in the afternoon and evening and be staffed with sufficient instructional personnel during those hours to supervise and assist with broad programs of independent study.

The first step in restructuring the school day is to replace year-long courses with semester length courses and even the semester course curriculum should contain a healthy sprinkling of single concept mini courses lasting no more than two or three weeks.

The intent of the restructured day is to make the working facilities of the school more easily accessible for use after school hours and in the evening and to free the student for service, work study, or field work during the day. In a time of great interest in learning, art studios, science laboratories and other inventive facilities must be planned, staffed, and equipped for easy accessibility and continuous use.

Access to learning is an important phrase and does not mean just a convenient arrangement of courses. It is an ease of mobility within the curriculum—not just an open facility, but a magnetic one as well. Access to learning is a totality of scope and execution that imbues the school curriculum with a dynamic spirit and force.

Recommendation No. 3:   The Restructured Week

Not only must the school day be restructured, but the school week as well must undergo just as serious a revision. In order for the school to take advantage of the comprehensive concepts of field work, service learning, and work training, the school week must be loosened and variegated.

For example, students should have the opportunity of pursuing the basic high school subjects three days a week, instead of the traditional five. Under this new flexibility a student can attend classes on Monday, Wednesday, and Friday, and engage in learning activities within the community on Tuesday and Thursday. A variation of this plan and perhaps a first step in moving to the restructured week is for students to attend classes on Monday, Tuesday, Thursday and Friday, and report for service activities, field work, or work study on Wonderful Wednesday.

Recommendation No. 4: Service Learning

High schools committed to comprehensiveness must expand their horizons and recognize that learning opportunities outside of the school are comparable, more appropriate, and often superior to activities arranged within the school.

Students should spend a decreasing amount of time at school and an increasing involvement in community service. The dimension of service comprises a broadening and tantalizing experience for the person who performs the activity.

The concept of service learning recognizes youth as an integral part of the community and establishes its importance to society. There should be no hard and fast rule as to the type of service which a student performs. The activity should be highly individualized and the only restriction should be that the activity be one of service in some observable way to an individual, agency, institution, or community.

An effect of students performing service to others is a transition from close supervision and hourly answerability of time to little supervision and a more flexible accountability which calls for more personal responsibility.

Recommendation No. 5: Work study

Every high school student needs the experience of working before leaving high school. Unrelated to vocational programs of career training, the school should accommodate this experience within the curriculum.

The easiest and most effective way of handling this is to give full high school credit for at least one semester's work on the job. After the schools have had experience with this arrangement for a while, they may want to expand work experience credit to a full school year.

Work experience is extremely valuable for young people and is one of the most maturing experiences that can happen to a high school student. The schools should no longer ignore this important adjunct to the curriculum but make it an important part of a broad comprehensive program of studies.

Recommendation No. 6: Contracted Vocational Education

All vocational education programs should operate in viable shops and businesses within the community instead of in the artificial atmosphere of simulation within the school. This is easily accomplished through the process of contracting with community businesses as training agencies.

Presently all comprehensive high schools have several shops, the most popular being auto mechanics, and these shops simulate the real thing. Since it is impossible for a high school to provide sufficient shops for the various trades in which its students are interested, this phase of the school program should be organized on a contract basis, with the school prepared to sign a contract for any type of vocational training available in the community. By contracting broadly, the school can offer a multitude of vocational opportunities and at the same time provide the students with more in-depth training than is possible in the presently existing simulated vocational shops housed within the school.

The contractual arrangement is also much less expensive than the present organization of vocational education which requires the school to build and maintain expensive shops which duplicate community facilities.

Recommendation No. 7: Foreign Languages

The New York Times recently devoted its Sunday educational supplement to the problem of teaching foreign languages. The issue was based upon a survey and study of what is being done in the schools.

The gist of the matter is that the teaching of foreign languages is in a serious state of intellectual disrepair, and as a result, a growing number of liberal arts colleges have eliminated foreign language as a requirement. These include Yale, Brown, Stanford, and a host of others.

The foreign language debacle was brought about by two factors: (1) The botching of teaching foreign languages in the elementary schools. Here schools would offer the language in a particular grade, say the third, but would not offer it in the fourth. It became a hit and miss affair with no continuity. (2) The introduction of the foreign language laboratory. This should have been a bright new heresy for individualized instruction, but unfortunately, the foreign language teachers used it in the same way they have used the textbook. Instead of allowing individual programs, they kept everybody in the same place on the tape at the same time just as in conventional classes where everyone was on the same page in the textbook.

Undergirding the mismanagement of teaching foreign languages is the continuing problem of the country's geographical isolation.

It is recommended that no student undertake foreign language study unless he plans to study it in depth. No credit should be given for less than three years of foreign language study. Less than this is a waste of the student's time, as he cannot communicate in the language, and he doesn't learn much about the culture of the country whose language he is studying.

Recommendation No. 8:   The Counseling System

In his book on the American High School, James B. Conant describes the functions of the counselor as "to supplement parental advice to a youngster." When counselors assume this function, they create another encroachment of the school on the home. Conant further advocated a broad extension of the counseling system. The problem is that he called for more of the same.

In the seventies the counseling system is in deep trouble. Parents have rejected the "supplementary" role; students are unhappy with the advice they get; and everybody agrees that counselors, both by training and performance, concentrate on the college bound and how to get this group into college. The career students who make up the great majority of the high schools' student bodies receive little or no help.

It is recommended that the traditional counseling system be abolished. It should be replaced by a system using for its personnel a consortium of teachers and business personnel. Every student should have a curriculum counselor to assist him with planning his in-school program and activities. This individual should have a teacher background. He should also have access to a career adviser. The career counselor should definitely not be an educator, but a business trained person capable of giving assistance with career objectives.

Recommendation No. 9:   A Nongraded Curriculum

The nongraded program of studies for high schools has been around since 1959, yet few schools have taken advantage of this innovative plan. Surprisingly, those that have, have all become great national models. Melbourne, Florida, High School; Trenton, Michigan, High School; Athens, Ohio, High School; and the Corsicana, Texas, High School have all acquired international reputations through their nongraded programs.

An important feature of the nongraded organization is its applicability to both small and large high schools. It is difficult to measure which school profits the most from the flexible nongraded arrangement, the small or the large, but the individual student wins in either and this is the point.

Colleges and universities are making increasing use of nongradedness through the Advanced Placement Program of the College Board as well as newer and more nontraditional approaches to flexibility.

It is recommended that all high schools adopt comprehensive nongraded, nontraditional type programs in order to better serve the nation's youth.

Recommmendation No. 10:   Independent Study

There is nothing quite so unequal as the equal treatment of unequals. No school will argue with this statement but most will respond with, "Yes, but some are more unequal than others." It is this response that has kept schools from developing highly individualized independent study programs.

Every high school faculty should adopt as a major goal the purpose of developing students who not only have learned how to learn, but are willing to accept responsibility for their own learning. Highly individualized independent learning opportunities should be open to all students who can handle themselves in learning situations which do not require pressure. Furthermore, independent study should begin as early as the student can cope with it.

The more able students should be privileged to elect almost completely independent programs and all students should have increasing but varying degrees of independence. The gist of the matter is that learning is something that people do for themselves, and we had best get on with it from that standpoint, shifting the schools' emphasis from teaching to learning.

Recommendation No. 11:   Field Work

As long as education is confined to the four walls of the school, it will remain narrow, and rigid. For education to be truly comprehensive, it must embrace all of the resources of the community.

In every discipline there are innumerable and kaleidoscopic opportunities for field work which the schools must use. For example, almost any aspect of biology or chemistry should relate to the ecological imbalance which exists in almost every community. Social studies courses must become heavily integrated with local government and the courts. Studies of court cases are much more realistic when viewed from the courtroom than when studied from a textbook. Government takes on new meaning when the city council is wrestling with a zoning change in which the pros and cons are about equally divided, as is usually the case.

One of the first happenings in any class should be an assessment of the field work opportunities in that particular discipline. This should be followed by planning how these propitious happenings can most effectively be integrated with class work.

Field work, in this setting, is far different from the traditionally existing system, where the youngsters take a field trip in search of biological specimens, or to ascertain, within a couple of hours, how the local government works.

Field work in the new comprehensive model refers to a clinical experience, from which the student acquires certain knowledge or skills, which he then demonstrates in another setting, such as the classroom. It is, in essence, serious laboratory work, related to a major concept or theory which he is studying in connection with his regular program of studies.

APPENDIX: The United States Supreme Court Argument and Decision in the Tinker Case

The famous Tinker case of the Supreme Court is printed in its entirety here for two reasons: (1) It is the basis for the new student freedoms in the schools, and in this capacity it is constantly being used to support a more liberal school policy. (2) Nowhere is the case easily available for educators. The Clerk of the Supreme Court reports that the Court's supply is exhausted and they do not plan to reprint. The Clerk feels that the responsibility for making the case generally available is now that of the U.S. Government Printing Office. The Printing Office advises that it has no plans for reprinting the decision.

Since this decision legally eliminated the concept of *in loco parentis,* which gave the teachers the right to stand in the place of the parent, and made school children persons under the constitution with all of the freedom of the Bill of Rights, then it has enormous implications for changing the entire structure of the schools as its tenets become more widely understood and integrated into school policy.

Every educator should have easy access to this important decision for ready reference as new questions of students' rights and privileges become an issue.

SUPREME COURT OF THE UNITED STATES

No. 21.—OCTOBER TERM, 1968.

John F. Tinker and Mary Beth Tinker, Minors, etc., et al., Petitioners, *v.* Des Moines Independent Community School District et al.	On Writ of Certiorari to the United States Court of Appeals for the Eighth Circuit.

[February 24, 1969.]

MR. JUSTICE FORTAS delivered the opinion of the Court.

Petitioner John F. Tinker, 15 years old, and petitioner Christopher Eckhardt, 16 years old, attended high schools in Des Moines. Petitioner Mary Beth Tinker, John's sister, was a 13-year-old student in junior high school.

In December 1965, a group of adults and students in Des Moines, Iowa, held a meeting at the Eckhardt home. The group determined to publicize their objections to the hostilities in Vietnam and their support for a truce by wearing black armbands during the holiday season and by fasting on December 16 and New Year's Eve. Petitioners and their parents had previously engaged in similar activities, and they decided to participate in the program.

The principals of the Des Moines schools became aware of the plan to wear armbands. On December 14, 1965, they met and adopted a policy that any student wearing an armband to school would be asked to remove it, and if he refused he would be suspended until he returned without the armband. Petitioners were aware of the regulation that the school authorities adopted.

On December 16, Mary Beth and Christopher wore black armbands to their schools. John Tinker wore his armband the next day. They were all sent home and suspended from school until they would come back without their armbands. They did not return to school until

after the planned period for wearing armbands had expired—that is, until after New Year's Day.

This complaint was filed in the United States District
Court by petitioners, through their fathers, under § 1983
of Title 42 of the United States Code. It prayed for an
injunction restraining the defendant school officials and
the defendant members of the board of directors of the
school district from disciplining the petitioners, and it
sought nominal damages. After an evidentiary hearing the District Court dismissed the complaint. It upheld the constitutionality of the school authorities' action
on the ground that it was reasonable in order to prevent
disturbance of school discipline. 258 F. Supp. 971
(1966). The court referred to but expressly declined
to follow the Fifth Circuit's holding in a similar case
that prohibition of the wearing of symbols like the armbands cannot be sustained unless it "materially and substantially interfere[s] with the requirements of appropriate discipline in the operation of the school." *Burnside*
v. *Byars,* 363 F. 2d 744, 749 (1966).[1]

On appeal, the Court of Appeals for the Eighth Circuit
considered the case *en banc.* The court was equally
divided, and the District Court's decision was accordingly affirmed, without opinion. 383 F. 2d 988 (1967).
We granted certiorari. 390 U. S. 942 (1968).

I.

The District Court recognized that the wearing of an
armband for the purpose of expressing certain views is

---

[1] In *Burnside,* the Fifth Circuit ordered that high school authorities be enjoined from enforcing a regulation forbidding students to
wear "freedom buttons." It is instructive that in *Blackwell* v.
Issaquena County Board of Education, 363 F. 2d 749 (1966), the
same panel on the same day reached the opposite result on different
facts. It declined to enjoin enforcement of such a regulation in
another high school where the students wearing freedom buttons
harassed students who did not wear them and created much
disturbance.

the type of symbolic act that is within the Free Speech
Clause of the First Amendment. See *West Virginia* v.
Barnette, 319 U. S. 624 (1943); *Stromberg* v. *California,*
283 U. S. 359 (1931). Cf. *Thornhill* v. *Alabama,* 310
U. S. 88 (1940); *Edwards* v. *South Carolina,* 372 U. S.
229 (1963); *Brown* v. *Louisiana,* 383 U. S. 131 (1966).
As we shall discuss, the wearing of armbands in the
circumstances of this case was entirely divorced from
actually or potentially disruptive conduct by those participating in it. It was closely akin to "pure speech"
which, we have repeatedly held, is entitled to comprehensive protection under the First Amendment. Compare *Cox* v. *Louisiana,* 379 U. S. 536, 555 (1965); *Adderley*
v. *Florida,* 385 U. S. 39 (1966).

First Amendment rights, applied in light of the
special characteristics of the school environment, are
available to teachers and students. It can hardly be
argued that either students or teachers shed their constitutional rights to freedom of speech or expression at
the schoolhouse gate. This has been the unmistakable
holding of this Court for almost 50 years. In *Meyer* v.
Nebraska, 262 U. S. 390 (1923), and *Bartels* v. *Iowa,*
262 U. S. 404 (1923), this Court, in opinions by Mr. Justice McReynolds, held that the Due Process Clause of
the Fourteenth Amendment prevents States from forbidding the teaching of a foreign language to young
students. Statutes to this effect, the Court held, uncon-
stitutionally interfere with the liberty of teacher, student,
and parent.[2] See also *Pierce* v. *Society of Sisters,* 268

---

[2] *Hamilton* v. *Regents of Univ. of Cal.,* 293 U. S. 245 (1934) is
sometimes cited for the broad proposition that the State may attach
conditions to attendance at a state university that require individuals to violate their religious convictions. The case involved dis-
missal of members of a religious denomination from a land grant
college for refusal to participate in military training. Narrowly
viewed, the case turns upon the Court's conclusion that merely
requiring a student to participate in school training in military

U. S. 510 (1925); *West Virginia* v. *Barnette,* 319 U. S.
624 (1943); *McCollum* v. *Board of Education,* 333 U. S.
203 (1948); *Wieman* v. *Updegraff,* 344 U. S. 183, 195
(1952) (concurring opinion); *Sweezy* v. *New Hampshire,*
354 U. S. 234 (1957); *Shelton* v. *Tucker,* 364 U. S. 479,
487 (1960); *Engel* v. *Vitale,* 370 U. S. 421 (1962);
Keyishian v. *Board of Regents,* 385 U. S. 589, 603 (1967);
Epperson v. *Arkansas,* 393 U. S. 97 (1968).

In *West Virginia* v. *Barnette, supra,* this Court held
that under the First Amendment, the student in public
school may not be compelled to salute the flag. Speaking through Mr. Justice Jackson, the Court said:

> "The Fourteenth Amendment, as now applied to
> the States, protects the citizen against the State
> itself and all of its creatures—Boards of Education
> not excepted. These have, of course, important,
> delicate, and highly discretionary functions, but none
> that they may not perform within the limits of the
> Bill of Rights. That they are educating the young
> for citizenship is reason for scrupulous protection of
> Constitutional freedoms of the individual, if we are
> not to strangle the free mind at its source and teach
> youth to discount important principles of our gov-
> ernment as mere platitudes." 319 U. S., at 637.

On the other hand, the Court has repeatedly emphasized the need for affirming the comprehensive authority

---

"science" could not conflict with his constitutionally protected freedom of conscience. The decision cannot be taken as establishing that
the State may impose and enforce any conditions that it chooses upon
attendance at public institutions of learning, however violative they
may be of fundamental constitutional guaranties. See, *e. g., West
Virginia* v. *Barnette,* 319 U. S. 624 (1943); *Dixon* v. *Alabama State
Bd. of Educ.,* 294 F. 2d 150 (C. A. 5th Cir. 1961); *Knight* v.
State Bd. of Educ., 200 F. Supp. 174 (D. C. M. D. Tenn. 1961);
Dickey v. *Alabama St. Bd. of Educ.,* 273 F. Supp. 613 (C. A. M. D.
Ala. 1967). See also Note, 73 Harv. L. Rev. 1595 (1960); Note, 81
Harv. L. Rev. 1045 (1968).

of the States and of school authorities, consistent with
fundamental constitutional safeguards, to prescribe and
control conduct in the schools. See *Epperson* v. *Arkansas, supra,* at 104; *Meyer* v. *Nebraska, supra,* at 402.
Our problem lies in the area where students in the exercise of First Amendment rights collide with the rules of
the school authorities.

II.

The problem presented by the present case does not
relate to regulation of the length of skirts or the type
of clothing, to hair style or deportment. Compare
Ferrell v. *Dallas Independent School District,* 392 F. 2d
697 (1968); *Pugsley* v. *Sellmeyer,* 158 Ark. 247, 250
S. W. 538 (1923). It does not concern aggressive, disruptive action or even group demonstrations. Our problem involves direct, primary First Amendment rights
akin to "pure speech."

The school officials banned and sought to punish petitioners for a silent, passive, expression of opinion, unaccompanied by any disorder or disturbance on the part of
petitioners. There is here no evidence whatever of petitioners' interference, actual or nascent, with the school's
work or of collision with the rights of other students
to be secure and to be let alone. Accordingly, this case
does not concern speech or action that intrudes upon the
work of the school or the rights of other students.

Only a few of the 18,000 students in the school system
wore the black armbands. Only five students were suspended for wearing them. There is no indication that
the work of the school or any class was disrupted. Outside the classrooms, a few students made hostile remarks
to the children wearing armbands, but there were no
threats or acts of violence on school premises.

The District Court concluded that the action of the
school authorities was reasonable because it was based
upon their fear of a disturbance from the wearing of the

armbands. But, in our system, undifferentiated fear or apprehension of disturbance is not enough to overcome the right to freedom of expression. Any departure from absolute regimentation may cause trouble. Any variation from the majority's opinion may inspire fear. Any word spoken, in class, in the lunchroom or on the campus, that deviates from the views of another person, may start an argument or cause a disturbance. But our Constitution says we must take this risk, *Terminiello* v. *Chicago*, 337 U. S. 1. (1959); and our history says that it is this sort of hazardous freedom—this kind of openness—that is the basis of our national strength and of the independence and vigor of Americans who grow up and live in this relatively permissive, often disputatious society.

In order for the State in the person of school officials to justify prohibition of a particular expression of opinion, it must be able to show that its action was caused by something more than a mere desire to avoid the discomfort and unpleasantness that always accompany an unpopular viewpoint. Certainly where there is no finding and no showing that the exercise of the forbidden right would "materially and substantially interfere with the requirements of appropriate discipline in the operation of the school," the prohibition cannot be sustained. *Burnside* v. *Byars, supra,* at 749.

In the present case, the District Court made no such finding, and our independent examination of the record fails to yield evidence that the school authorities had reason to anticipate that the wearing of the armbands would substantially interfere with the work of the school or impinge upon the rights of other students. Even an official memorandum prepared after the suspension that listed the reasons for the ban on wearing the armbands made no reference to the anticipation of such disruption.[3]

---

[3] The only suggestions of fear of disorder in the report are these: "A former student of one of our high schools was killed in Viet

On the contrary, the action of the school authorities appears to have been based upon an urgent wish to avoid the controversy which might result from the expression, even by the silent symbol of armbands, of opposition to this Nation's part in the conflagration in Vietnam.[4] It is revealing, in this respect, that the meeting at which the school principals decided to issue the contested regulation was called in response to a student's statement to the journalism teacher in one of the schools that he wanted to write an article on Vietnam and have it published in the school paper. (The student was dissuaded.)[5]

Nam. Some of his friends are still in school and it was felt that if any kind of a demonstration existed, it might evolve into something which would be difficult to control.

"Students at one of the high schools were heard to say they would wear arm bands of other colors if the black bands prevailed."

Moreover, the testimony of school authorities at trial indicates that it was not fear of disruption that motivated the regulation prohibiting the armbands; the regulation was directed against "the principle of the demonstration" itself. School authorities simply felt that "the schools are no place for demonstrations," and if the students "didn't like the way our elected officials were handling things, it should be handled with the ballot box and not in the halls of our public schools."

[4] The District Court found that the school authorities, in prohibiting black armbands, were influenced by the fact that "[t]he Viet Nam war and the involvement of the United States therein has been the subject of a major controversy for some time. When the armband regulation involved herein was promulgated, debate over the Viet Nam war had become vehement in many localities. A protest march against the war had been recently held in Washington, D. C. A wave of draft-card-burning incidents protesting the war had swept the country. At that time two publicized draft burning were pending in this Court. Both individuals supporting the war and those opposing it were quite vocal in expressing their views." 258 F. Supp., at 972–973.

[5] After the principals' meeting, the director of secondary education and the principal of the high school informed the student that the principals were opposed to publication of his article. They

It is also relevant that the school authorities did not purport to prohibit the wearing of all symbols of political or controversial significance. The record shows that students in some of the schools wore buttons relating to national political campaigns, and some even wore the Iron Cross, traditionally a symbol of nazism. The order prohibiting the wearing of armbands did not extend to these. Instead, a particular symbol—black armbands worn to exhibit opposition to this Nation's involvement in Vietnam—was singled out for prohibition. Clearly, the prohibition of expression of one particular opinion, at least without evidence that it is necessary to avoid material and substantial interference with school work or discipline, is not constitutionally permissible.

In our system, state-operated schools may not be enclaves of totalitarianism. School officials do not possess absolute authority over their students. Students in school as well as out of school are "persons" under our Constitution. They are possessed of fundamental rights which the State must respect, just as they themselves must respect their obligations to the State. In our system, students may not be regarded as closed-circuit recipients of only that which the State chooses to communicate. They may not be confined to the expression of those sentiments that are officially approved. In the absence of a specific showing of constitutionally valid reasons to regulate their speech, students are entitled to freedom of expression of their views. As Judge Gewin, speaking for the Fifth Circuit said, school officials cannot suppress "expressions of feelings with which they do not wish to contend." *Burnside* v. *Byars, supra,* at 749.

---

reported that "we felt that it was a very friendly conversation, although we did not feel that we had convinced the student that our decision was a just one."

In *Meyer* v. *Nebraska, supra,* at 402, Justice McReynolds expressed this Nation's repudiation of the principle
that a State might so conduct its schools as to "foster
a homogeneous people."   He said:

> "In order to submerge the individual and develop
> ideal citizens, Sparta assembled the males at seven
> into barracks and intrusted their subsequent educa-
> tion and training to official guardians.   Although
> such measures have been deliberately approved by
> men of great genius, their ideas touching the rela-
> tion between individual and State were wholly dif-
> ferent from those upon which our institutions rest;
> and it hardly will be affirmed that any legislature
> could impose such restrictions upon the people of a
> State without doing violence to both letter and spirit
> of the Constitution."

This principle has been repeated by this Court on numerous occasions during the intervening years.   In *Keyishian*
v. *Board of Regents,* 385 U. S. 589, 603, MR. JUSTICE
BRENNAN, speaking for the Court, said:

> " 'The vigilant protection of constitutional freedom
> is nowhere more vital than in the community of
> American schools.'   *Shelton* v. *Tucker,* 234 U. S. 479,
> 487.   The classroom is peculiarly the 'market-place
> of ideas.'   The Nation's future depends upon leaders
> trained through wide exposure to that robust ex-
> change of ideas which discovers truth 'out of a multi-
> tude of tongues, [rather] than through any kind of
> authoritative selection' . . . ."

The principle of these cases is not confined to the supervised and ordained discussion which takes place in
the classroom.   The principal use to which the schools
are dedicated is to accommodate students during prescribed hours for the purpose of certain types of activities.

Among those activities is personal intercommunication among the students.[6] This is not only an inevitable part of the process of attending school. It is also an important part of the educational process. A student's rights therefore, do not embrace merely the classroom hours. When he is in the cafeteria, or on the playing field, or on the campus during the authorized hours, he may express his opinions, even on controversial subjects like the conflict in Vietnam, if he does so "without materially and substantially interfering with appropriate discipline in the operation of the school" and without colliding with the rights of others. *Burnside* v. *Byars, supra,* at 749. But conduct by the student, in class or out of it, which for any reason—whether it stems from time, place, or type of behavior—materially disrupts classwork or involves substantial disorder or invasion of the rights of others is, of course, not immunized by the constitutional guaranty of freedom of speech. Cf. *Blackwell* v. *Issaquena City Bd. of Educ.,* 363 F. 2d 749 (C. A. 5th Cir., 1966).

Under our Constitution, free speech is not a right that is given only to be so circumscribed that it exists in principle but not in fact. Freedom of expression would not truly exist if the right could be exercised only in an area that a benevolent government has provided as a safe haven for crackpots. The Constitution says that Congress (and the States) may not abridge the right to free

---

[6] In *Hammond* v. *South Carolina State College,* 272 F. Supp. 947 (D. C. D. S. C. 1967), District Judge Hemphill had before him a case involving a meeting on campus of 300 students to express their views on school practices. He pointed out that a school is not like a hospital or a jail enclosure. Cf. *Cox* v. *Louisiana,* 379 U. S. 536 (1965); *Adderley* v. *Florida,* 385 U. S. 39 (1966). It is a public place, and its dedication to specific uses does not imply that the constitutional rights of persons entitled to be there are to be gauged as if the premises were purely private property. Cf. *Edwards* v. *South Carolina,* 372 U. S. 229 (1963); *Brown* v. *Louisiana,* 383 U. S. 131 (1966).

speech. This provision means what it says. We properly read it to permit reasonable regulation of speech-
connected activities in carefully restricted circumstances.
But we do not confine the permissible exercise of First
Amendment rights to a telephone booth or the four
corners of a pamphlet, or to supervised and ordained
discussion in a school classroom.

If a regulation were adopted by school officials forbidding discussion of the Vietnam conflict, or the expression by any student of opposition to it anywhere on
school property except as part of a prescribed classroom exercise, it would be obvious that the regulation
would violate the constitutional rights of students, at
least if it could not be justified by a showing that the
students' activities would materially and substantially
disrupt the work and discipline of the school. Cf. *Hammond* v. *South Carolina State College,* 272 F. Supp. 947
(D. C. D. S. C. 1967) (orderly protest meeting on state
college campus); *Dickey* v. *Alabama State Board,* 273 F.
Supp. 613 (D. C. M. D. Ala. 1967) (expulsion of student
editor of college newspaper). In the circumstances of
the present case, the prohibition of the silent, passive
"witness of the armbands," as one of the children called
it, is no less offensive to the Constitution's guaranties.

As we have discussed, the record does not demonstrate
any facts which might reasonably have led school authorities to forecast substantial disruption of or material interference with school activities, and no disturbances or
disorders on the school premises in fact occurred. These
petitioners merely went about their ordained rounds in
school. Their deviation consisted only in wearing on
their sleeve a band of black cloth, not more than two
inches wide. They wore it to exhibit their disapproval
of the Vietnam hostilities and their advocacy of a truce, to
make their views known, and by their example, to influence others to adopt them. They neither interrupted

school activities nor sought to intrude in the school affairs
or the lives of others. They caused discussion outside
of the classrooms, but no interference with work and no
disorder. In the circumstances, our Constitution does
not permit officials of the State to deny their form of
expression.

We express no opinion as to the form of relief which
should be granted, this being a matter for the lower courts
to determine. We reverse and remand for further pro-
ceedings consistent with this opinion.

Reversed and remanded.

SUPREME COURT OF THE UNITED STATES

No. 21.—October Term, 1968.

John F. Tinker and Mary Beth
Tinker, Minors, etc., et al.,
Petitioners,
v.
Des Moines Independent Community School District et al.

On Writ of Certiorari to the United States Court of Appeals for the Eighth Circuit.

[February 24, 1969.]

Mr. Justice Stewart, concurring.

Although I agree with much of what is said in the Court's opinion, and with its judgment in this case, I cannot share the Court's uncritical assumption that, school discipline aside, the First Amendment rights of children are co-extensive with those of adults. Indeed, I had thought the Court decided otherwise just last Term in *Ginsberg* v. *New York*, 390 U. S. 629. I continue to hold the view I expressed in that case: "[A] State may permissibly determine that, at least in some precisely delineated areas, a child—like someone in a captive audience—is not possessed of that full capacity for individual choice which is the presupposition of First Amendment guarantees." *Id.*, at 649–650 (concurring opinion). Cf. *Prince* v. *Massachusetts*, 321 U. S. 158.

SUPREME COURT OF THE UNITED STATES

No. 21.—OCTOBER TERM, 1968.

| John F. Tinker and Mary Beth Tinker, Minors, etc., et al., Petitioners, v. Des Moines Independent Community School District et al. | On Writ of Certiorari to the United States Court of Appeals for the Eighth Circuit. |

[February 24, 1969.]

MR. JUSTICE WHITE, concurring.

While I join the Court's opinion, I deem it appropriate to note, first, that the Court continues to recognize a distinction between communicating by words and communicating by acts or conduct which sufficiently impinge on some valid state interest; and, second, that I do not subscribe to everything the Court of Appeals said about free speech in its opinion in *Burnside* v. *Byars,* 363 F. 2d 744, 748 (C. A. 5th Cir. 1966), a case relied upon by the Court in the matter now before us.

SUPREME COURT OF THE UNITED STATES

No. 21.—OCTOBER TERM, 1968.

John F. Tinker and Mary Beth Tinker, Minors, etc., et al., Petitioners, *v.* Des Moines Independent Community School District et al.	On Writ of Certiorari to the United States Court of Appeals for the Eighth Circuit.

[February 24, 1969.]

Mr. JUSTICE BLACK, dissenting.

The Court's holding in this case ushers in what I deem to be an entirely new era in which the power to control pupils by the elected "officials of state supported public schools . . ." in the United States is in ultimate effect transferred to the Supreme Court.[1] The Court brought this particular case here on a petition for certiorari urging that the First and Fourteenth Amendments protect the right of schools pupils to express their political views all the way "from kindergarten through high school."   Here the constitutional right to "political expression" asserted was a right to wear black armbands during school hours and at classes in order to demonstrate to the other students that the petitioners were mourning because of the death of United States' soldiers in Vietnam and to protest that war which they were against.   Ordered to refrain from wearing the armbands in school by the elected school officials and the teachers vested with state authority to do so, apparently only seven out of the school system's 18,000 pupils deliberately refused

---

[1] The petition for certiorari here presented this single question:
"Whether the First and Fourteenth Amendments permit officials of state-supported public schools to prohibit students from wearing symbols of political views within school premises where the symbols are not disruptive of school discipline or decorum."

to obey the order. One defying pupil was Paul Tinker, 8 years old, who was in the second grade; another, Hope Tinker was 11 years old in the fifth grade; a third member of the Tinker family was 13, in the eighth grade; and a fourth member of the same family was John Tinker, 15 years old, an 11th grade high school pupil. Their father, a Methodist minister without a church, is paid a salary by the American Friends Service Committee. Another student who defied the school order and insisted on wearing an armband in school was Chris Eckhardt, an 11th grade pupil and a petitioner in this case. His mother is an official in the Women's International League for Peace and Freedom.

As I read the Court's opinion it relies upon the following grounds for holding unconstitutional the judgment of the Des Moines school officials and the two Courts below. First the Court concludes that the wearing of armbands is "symbolic speech" which is "akin to pure speech" and therefore protected by the First and Fourteenth Amendments. Secondly, the Court decides that the public schools are an appropriate place to exercise "symbolic speech" as long as normal school functions are not "unreasonably" disrupted. Finally, the Court arrogates to itself, rather than to the State's elected officials charged with running the schools, the decision as to which school disciplinary regulations are "reasonable."

Assuming that the Court is correct in holding that the conduct of wearing armbands for the purpose of conveying political ideas is protected by the First Amendment compare, e. g., *Giboney* v. *Empire Storage & Ice Co.*, 336 U. S. 490 (1949), the crucial remaining questions are whether students and teachers may use the schools at their whim as a platform for the exercise of free speech—"symbolic" or "pure"—and whether the Courts will allocate to themselves the function of deciding how the pupils school day will be spent. While I have always believed that under the First and Fourteenth Amendments neither the State nor Federal Government has any authority to regulate or censor the content of speech, I have never believed that any person has a right to give speeches or engage in demonstrations where he pleases and when he pleases. This Court has already rejected such a notion. In *Cox* v. *Louisiana,* 379 U. S. 536 (1964), for example, the Court clearly stated that the rights of free speech and assembly "do not mean that anyone with opinions or beliefs to express may address a group at any public place and at any time." 379 U. S. 536, 554 (1964).

While the record does not show that any of these armband students shouted, used profane language or were violent in any manner, a detailed report by some of them shows their armbands caused comments, warnings by other students, the poking of fun at them, and a warning by an older football player that other, non-protesting students had better let them alone. There is also evidence that the professor of mathematics had his lesson period practically "wrecked" chiefly by disputes with Beth Tinker, who wore her armband for her "demonstration." Even a casual reading of the record shows that this armband did divert students' minds from their regular lessons, and that talk, comments, etc., made John Tinker "self-conscious" in attending school with his armband. While the absence of obscene or boisterous and loud disorder perhaps justifies the Court's statement that the few armband students did not actually "disrupt" the classwork, I think the record overwhelmingly shows that the armbands did exactly what the elected school officials and principals foresaw it would, that is, took the students' minds off their classwork and diverted them to thoughts about the highly emotional subject of the Vietnam war. And I repeat that if the time has come when pupils of state-supported schools, kindergarten, grammar school or high school, can defy and flaunt orders of school officials to keep their minds on their own school work, it is the beginning of a new revolutionary era of permissiveness in this country fostered by the judiciary. The next logical step, it appears to me, would be to hold unconstitutional laws that bar pupils under 21 or 18 from voting, or from being elected members of the Boards of Education.[2]

The United States District Court refused to hold that the State school orders violated the First and Fourteenth Amendments. 258 F. Supp. 971. Holding that the protest was akin to speech, which is protected by the First and Fourteenth Amendments, that court held that the school orders were "reasonable" and hence constitutional. There was at one time a line of cases holding "reasonableness" as the court saw it to be the test of a "due process" violation. Two cases upon which the the Court today heavily relies for striking down these school orders used this test of reasonableness, *Meyers* v. *Nebraska*, 262 U. S. 390 (1923) and *Bartells* v. *Iowa*, 262 U. S. 404 (1923). The opinions in both cases were written by Mr. Justice McReynolds; Mr. Justice Holmes, who opposed this reasonableness test, dissented from the holdings as did Mr. Justice Sutherland. This constitutional test of reasonableness prevailed in this Court for a season.

---

[2] The following Associated Press article appeared in the Washington *Evening Star*, January 11, 1969, p. A–2, col. 1.

"BELLINGHAM, Mass. (AP)—Todd R. Hennessy, 16, has filed nominating papers to run for town park commissioner in the March election.

" 'I can see nothing illegal in the youth's seeking the elective office,' said Lee Ambler, the town counsel. 'But I can't overlook the possibility that if he is elected any legal contract entered into by the park commissioner would be void because he is a juvenile.'

"Todd is a junior in Mount St. Charles Academy, where he has a top scholastic record."

It was this test that brought on President Franklin Roosevelt's well-known Court fight. His proposed legislation did not pass, but the fight left the "reasonable" constitutional test dead on the battlefield, so much so that this Court in *Ferguson* v. *Skrupa,* 372 U. S. 726, 729, 730, after a thorough review of the old cases, was able to conclude in 1962:

> "There was a time when the Due Process Clause was used by this Court to strike down laws which were thought unreasonable, that is, unwise or incompatible with some economic or social philosophy . . . . The doctrine that prevailed in *Lochner, Coppage, Adkins, Burns,* and like cases—that due process authorizes courts to hold laws unconstitutional when they believe the legislature has acted unwisely—has long since been discarded."

The *Ferguson* case totally repudiated the old reasonableness due process test, the doctrine that judges have the power to hold laws unconstitutional upon the belief of judges that they are "unreasonable," "arbitrary," "shock the conscience," "irrational," "contrary to fundamental 'deceny,'" or some other such flexible term without precise boundaries. I have many times expressed my opposition to that concept on the ground that it gives judges power to strike down any law they do not like. If the majority of the Court today, by agreeing to the opinion of my Brother FORTAS, is resurrecting that old reasonableness due process test, I think the constitutional change should be plainly, unequivocally, and forthrightly stated for the benefit of the bench and bar. It will be a sad day for the country, I believe, when the present day Court returns to the McReynolds' due process concept. Other cases cited by the Court do not, as implied, follow the McReynolds' reasonableness doctrine. *West Virginia* v. *Barnette,* 319 U. S. 625, clearly rejecting the "reasonableness" test, held that the Fourteenth Amendment made the First applicable to the States, and held that the two forbade a State to *compel* little school children to salute the United States flag when they had religious scruples against it.[3]   Neither *Thornhill* v. *Alabama,* 310 U. S. 88; *Stromberg* v. *California,* 283 U. S. 359; *Edwards* v. *South Carolina,* 372 U. S. 329, nor *Brown* v. *Louisiana,* 382 U. S. 131, related to school children at all, and none of these cases embraced Mr. Justice McReynolds' reasonableness test; and *Thornhill, Edwards,* and *Brown* relied on the vagueness of state statutes under scrutiny to hold it unconstitutional. *Cox* v. *Louisiana,* 379 U. S. 536, 555, and *Adderley* v. *Florida,* 385 U. S. 39, cited by the Court as a "compare," indicating, I suppose, that these two cases are no longer the law, were not rested to the slightest extent on the *Meyers* and *Bartell* "reasonableness-due process-McReynolds'" constitutional test.

I deny, therefore, that it has been the "unmistakable holding of this Court for almost 50 years" that "students" and "teachers" take with them into the "schoolhouse gate" constitutional rights to "freedom of speech or

---

[3] In *Cantwell* v. *Connecticut,* 310 U. S. 296, 303–304 (1939), this Court said:

"The First Amendment declares that Congress shall make no law respecting an establishment of religion or prohibiting the free exercise thereof. The Fourteenth Amendment has rendered the legislatures of the states as incompetent as Congress to enact such laws. The constitutional inhibition of legislation on the subject of religion has a double aspect. On the one hand, it forestalls compulsion by law of the acceptance of any creed or the practice of any form of worship. Freedom of conscience and freedom to adhere to such religious organization or form of worship as the individual may choose cannot be restricted by law. On the other hand, it safeguards the free exercise of the chosen form of religion. Thus the Amendment embraces two concepts—freedom to believe and freedom to act. The first is absolute but, in the nature of things, the second cannot be. Conduct remains subject to regulation for the protection of society."

expression." Even *Meyer* did not hold that. It makes
no reference to "symbolic speech" at all; what it did
was to strike down as "unreasonable" and therefore
unconstitutional a Nebraska law barring the teaching
of the German language before the children reached
their eighth grade. One can well agree with Justice
Holmes and Mr. Justice Sutherland, as I do, that
such a law was no more unreasonable than it would
be to bar the teaching of Latin and Greek to pupils who
have not reached the eighth grade. In fact, I think the
majority's reason for invalidating the Nebraska law was
that they did not like or in legal jargon that it "shocked
the Court's conscience," "offended its sense of justice"
was "contrary to fundamental concepts of the English-
speaking world," as the Court has sometimes said. See,
e. g., Rochin v. *California,* 342 U. S. 165, and *Irvine* v.
California, 347 U. S. 128. The truth is that a teacher
of kindergarten, grammar school, or high school pupils
no more carries into a school with him a complete right
to freedom of speech and expression than an anti-Catholic
or anti-Semitic carries with him a complete freedom of
speech and religion into a Catholic church or Jewish
synagogue. Nor does a person carry with him into the
United States Senate or House, or to the Supreme Court,
or any other court, a complete constitutional right to go
into those places contrary to their rules and speak his
mind on any subject he pleases. It is a myth to say that
any person has a constitutional right to say what he
pleases, where he pleases, and when he pleases. Our
Court has decided precisely the opposite. See, *e. g.,*
Cox v. *Louisiana,* 379 U. S. 536, 555; *Adderley* v. *Florida,*
385 U. S. 39.

In my view, teachers in state-controlled public schools
are hired to teach there. Although Mr. Justice McReynolds may have intimated to the contrary in *Meyers* v.
Nebraska, supra, certainly a teacher is not paid to go into

school and teach subjects the State does not hire him to teach as a part of its selected curriculum. Nor are public school students sent to the schools at public expense to broadcast political or any other views to educate and inform the public. The original idea of schools, which I do not believe is yet abandoned as worthless or out of date, was that children had not yet reached the point of experience and wisdom which enabled them to teach all of their elders. It may be that the Nation has outworn the old-fashioned slogan that "children are to be seen not heard," but one may, I hope, be permitted to harbor the thought that taxpayers send children to school on the premise that at their age they need to learn, not teach.

The true principles on this whole subject were in my judgment spoken by Mr. Justice McKenna for the Court in *Waugh* v. *Mississippi University* in 237 U. S. 589, 596–597. The State had there passed a law barring students from peaceably assembling in Greek letter fraternities and providing that students who joined them could be expelled from school. This law would appear on the surface to run afoul of the First Amendment's freedom of assembly clause. The law was attacked as violative of due process and as a deprivation of property, of liberty, and of the privileges and immunities clause of the Fourteenth Amendment. It was argued that the fraternity made its members more moral, taught discipline, and inspired its members to study harder and to obey better the rules of discipline and order. This Court rejected all the "fervid" pleas of the fraternities' advocates decided unanimously against these Fourteenth Amendment arguments. The Court in its closing paragraph made this statement which has complete relevance for us today:

"It is said that the fraternity to which complainant belongs is a moral and of itself a disciplinary force. This need not be denied. But whether such mem-

bership makes against discipline was for the State
of Mississippi to determine. It is to be remem-
bered that the University was established by the
State and is under the control of the State, and the
enactment of the statute may have been induced by
the opinion that *membership in the prohibited societies divided the attention of the students and distracted from that singleness of purpose which the
State desired to exist in its public educational institutions.* It is not for us to entertain conjectures in
opposition to the views of the State and annul its
regulations upon disputable considerations of their
wisdom or necessity." (Emphasis supplied.)

It was on the foregoing argument that this Court
sustained the power of Mississippi to curtail the First
Amendment's right of peaceable assembly. And the
same reasons are equally applicable to curtailing in the
States' public schools the right to complete freedom of
expression. Iowa's public schools, like Mississippi's university, are operated to give students an opportunity to
learn, not to talk politics by actual speech, or by "symbolic" speech. And as I have pointed out before, the
record amply shows that public protest in the school
classes against the Vietnam war "distracted from that
singleness of purpose which the State (here Iowa)
desired to exist in its public educational institutions."
Here the Court should accord Iowa educational institutions the same right to determine for itself what free
expression and no more should be allowed in its schools
that it accorded Mississippi with reference to freedom
of assembly. But even if the record were silent as to
protests against the Vietnam war distracting students
from their assigned class work, members of this Court,
like all other citizens, know, without being told, that
the disputes over the wisdom of the Vietnam war have
disrupted and divided this country as few other issues

ever have. Of course students, like other people, cannot concentrate on lesser issues when black armbands are being ostentatiously displayed in their presence to call attention to the wounded and dead of the war, some of the wounded and the dead being their friends and neighbors. It was, of course, to distract the attention of other students that some students insisted up to the very point of their own suspension from school that they were determined to sit in school with their symbolic armbands.

Change has been said to be truly the law of life but sometimes the old and the tried and true are worth holding. The schools of this Nation have undoubtedly contributed to giving us tranquility and to making us a more law-abiding people. Uncontrolled and uncontrolable liberty is an enemy to domestic peace. We cannot close our eyes to the fact that some of the country's greatest problems are crimes committed by the youth, too many of school age. School discipline, like parental discipline, is an integral and important part of training our children to be good citizens—to be better citizens. Here a very small number of students have crisply and summarily refused to obey a school order designed to give pupils who want to learn the opportunity to do so. One does not need to be a prophet or the son of a prophet to know that after the Court's holding today that some students in Iowa schools and indeed in all schools will be ready, able, and willing to defy their teachers on practically all orders. This is the more unfortunate for the schools since groups of students all over the land are already running loose, conducting break-ins, sit-ins, lie-ins, and smash-ins. Many of these student groups, as is all too familiar to all who read the newspapers and watch the television news programs, have already engaged in rioting, property seizures and destruction. They have picketed schools to force students not to cross their picket lines and have too often violently attacked earnest but frightened students who wanted an education that the picketers did not want them to get. Students engaged in such activities are apparently confident that they know far more about how to operate public school systems than do their parents, teachers, and elected school officials. It is no answer to say that the particular students here have not yet reached such high points in their demands to attend classes in order to exercise their political pressures. Turned loose with law suits for damages and injunctions against their teachers like they are here, it is nothing but wishful thinking to imagine that young, immature students will not soon believe it is their right to control the schools rather than the right of the States that collect the taxes to hire the teachers for the benefit of the pupils. This case, therefore, wholly without constitutional reasons in my judgment, subjects all the public schools in the country to the whims and caprices of their loudest-mouthed, but maybe not their brightest, students. I, for one, am not fully persuaded that school pupils are wise enough, even with this Court's expert help from Washington, to run the 23,390 public school systems [4] in our 50 States. I wish, therefore, wholly to disclaim any purpose on my part, to hold that the Federal Constitution compels the teachers, parents, and elected school officials to surrender control of the American public school system to public school students. I dissent.

---

[4] Statistical Abstract of the United States (1968), Table No. 578, p. 406.

SUPREME COURT OF THE UNITED STATES

No. 21.—OCTOBER TERM, 1968.

John F. Tinker and Mary Beth Tinker, Minors, etc., et al., Petitioners, *v.* Des Moines Independent Community School District et al.	On Writ of Certiorari to the United States Court of Appeals for the Eighth Circuit.

[February 24, 1969.]

MR. JUSTICE HARLAN, dissenting.

I certainly agree that state public school authorities in the discharge of their responsibilities are not wholly exempt from the requirements of the Fourteenth Amendment respecting the freedoms of expression and association. At the same time I am reluctant to believe that there is any disagreement between the majority and myself on the proposition that school officials should be accorded the widest authority in maintaining discipline and good order in their institutions. To translate that proposition into a workable constitutional rule, I would, in cases like this, cast upon those complaining the burden of showing that a particular school measure was motivated by other than legitimate school concerns—for example, a desire to prohibit the expression of an unpopular point of view, while permitting expression of the dominant opinion.

Finding nothing in this record which impugns the good faith of respondents in promulgating the arm band regulation, I would affirm the judgment below.

INDEX